Will to Endure

Surviving Terminal Illness by
Extraordinary Means

A Memoir

John L'Esperance

ISBN-10: 0615890628
ISBN-13: 9780615890623

For my son, Garth, who continues to be the center of my universe

THE AUTHOR WISHES to acknowledge the following individuals without whose assistance this book would not have been possible:

Carole L. Glickfeld, for her keen editorial insight.

My dear cousin, Mary Wiegenstein, for the pivotal role she's played in my extraordinary journey through her loving support, intelligence and metaphysical tutelage.

Those friends who stood by me through thick and through thin.

Joao Texeira de Farias, for his selfless mission which has allowed me and countless others the blessing of continued life.

The divine Spirit Entities of the Casa de Dom Inacio, without whom I would have remained stubbornly unconscious my entire life.

Table Of Contents

Preface

THIS BOOK BEGAN life as a journal shortly after I received my death sentence. I had A.L.S....Lou Gehrig's Disease...a progressively debilitating, fatal malady without treatment or cure. Based on how my symptoms first developed my neurologist told me I might survive as long as two years beyond diagnosis...if I was lucky. In a terror-stricken attempt to comprehend the mad jumble of thoughts and feelings coursing through my mind and heart I began keeping a detailed log. I was trying to stay sane as my health began to deteriorate. Keeping a journal provided a measure of calm and soothed my frayed nerves. At that point in time writing a book was the last thing on my mind.

I immediately began searching for an alternative to my death sentence. Time was not on my side. Every lead I explored turned out to be a mirage...seeming to offer promise at first glance only to dissolve upon closer scrutiny. Until one day my cousin showed me an article about a Brazilian healer who'd had astonishing results curing diseases as hopeless as mine. Something deep inside of me *knew* this was the right path to take. Since my initial foray to Brazil to see him in action for myself I've made almost yearly pilgrimages to the healing center where he works to receive treatment for my incurable condition.

As the years rolled by my diary swelled with detailed descriptions of what transpired at that extraordinary site along with other strange, new phenomena which began happening to me. My life became a continuous stream of one transcendent experience after another. In each of these instances something profound was shown to me. My life lessons were illuminated and, often, I was admonished for being lazy by spirit guides who suddenly began communicating with me. I was shown how to enter non-ordinary reality and gradually I became adept at accessing important information located there. At first it felt surreal as if I was dreaming, that I'd soon wakeup and discover what I'd undergone wasn't real. Yet after repeated episodes I came to understand that what I was being offered in these awe-inspiring encounters was a remarkable gift of insight, a profound blessing and a spiritual summons to do the work I came here to accomplish.

The greatest problem I faced writing this book lay in how to describe the incomparable experiences that were happening to me in an understandable vernacular. I discovered that although my extrasensory odysseys were comprehensible experientially they were much less easily grasped inside the confining boundaries of language. Supernatural phenomena, by definition, lie outside the realm of ready explanation. I found the answer to this conundrum by reading how other spiritual explorers before me portrayed their own rendezvous within non-ordinary reality. Still, it was up to me to find my own numinous idiom with which to depict the breadth of what I'd lived through.

Since that first tentative, fear-laden journal entry to present day seventeen years have come and gone. I first decided to write a book about four years after being diagnosed as wonder at my continuance intersected with deep gratitude. It took all the intervening time to fashion this book into its present day form. Like the journal that formed its foundation this book started out as a coping tool, a catharsis, a means of understanding what was happening to me. As my journey unfolded my journal started to become more than simply a means of self-purgation. It became a roadmap I could offer others who find themselves in dire straits health-wise with nowhere to turn. As my personal transformation unfolded I slowly evolved through my own efforts and out of necessity...all guided by unprecedented means.

This book metamorphosed in corresponding fashion. It's been a faithful, instructive companion for many years gestating to the point that it can finally be born. May it now provide you with a journey into unparalleled realms few ever glimpse.

John L'Esperance
January 2014

1

The News

IT HAD ALL begun innocuously enough. I'd noticed a slight catch develop in my voice but dismissed it as a by-product of the stress that seemed a ubiquitous facet of my go-go existence. As a busy, successful real estate broker and investor, my time was increasingly not my own. The price exacted from having built my business into a thriving enterprise was, beyond the accolades of my clientele and the sweet fruit of monetary rewards, a frenetic world to which I'd become a slave. Using my voice was an integral component of that equation. Now that taken-for-granted tool seemed to be in jeopardy.

When a friend jokingly asked me one afternoon if the slight slur in my speech was due to my having been drinking, I realized the problem had become obvious to others. In my stubborn ostrich-like attempts to compensate for the glitch in my vocal operating system, I'd tried altering my inflection. The ruse was successful for a few short months before I was forced to confront the increasingly querulous looks of family, friends and clients who, hearing the steadily advancing break in my voice, wondered what was amiss. By then there was no longer any hiding from the truth.

When I'd finally mustered the courage to enter the sterile, foreboding building that housed my neurologist's office a clammy sweat had broken out on the palms of my hands. On that cold November day I briefly considered staying in the coziness of my warm car. Yet I knew I had to get on with the process of finding answers. After the better part of a year spent consulting with a series of neurologists, enduring innumerable tests and receiving only quizzical looks in response to my puzzling new symptoms I was long overdue for any concrete and tangible information about exactly what was wrong with me. I was also well aware whatever had so far stumped these specialists could only mean the eventual diagnosis would be very serious to have systematically eluded their experienced, probing scrutiny. I tried to block this chilling thought from my mind as I entered the doctor's office and waited for her to meet me to review the results of the latest battery of tests.

While I waited for the physician I sat in a low-slung armchair and tried to occupy my mind with a sports magazine. I remember seeing pictures of behemoth football linemen looming menacingly on the page and wondering why they seemed like some robotic androids far removed from their proper place in a science fiction movie.

Manifesting a physical ailment that so far had thwarted the medical community's best efforts to name it had been surreal. I'd been functioning in a fog bank for many months now. After completing my work assignments like an automaton, I'd return home where wonder and worry captured even more of my attention as the scope of the growing problem was allowed space to fester unchecked by other thoughts. Sitting in the doctor's office with only the hum of the fluorescent lights to distract my anxious thoughts I couldn't begin to fathom how the next few minutes would change my life forever.

As the doctor entered the room I tried to glean the severity of the news from her facial expression and body language. But her business-like demeanor successfully masked any emotions she may have been feeling. She sat down in a chair next to me and after the superficial small talk explained she'd finally been able to come up with a name to attach to my mysterious symptoms. She said, "John, you have amyotrophic lateral sclerosis."

I didn't move for a moment. Her words didn't fully register at first. Sure, I'd heard of this illness but knew virtually nothing about it. After a brief pause I asked her what the treatment was for the disease she'd just named, intent on resolving the issue, having my voice restored and getting on with my busy life.

She gazed at me consolingly and, mustering a compassionate tone, explained there wasn't any treatment, that it was simply... incurable. She proceeded to describe the progressively increasing debilitation that is the central hallmark of the illness. I swallowed hard and felt my mouth go dry. My pulse began to race and the pounding in my chest threatened to rip me apart. I remember feeling the first traces of nausea overtake me as I sought to maintain composure. "What do you mean it's incurable?" I barked out through my fear-laced incredulity. She explained that there simply wasn't any treatment. She described the handful of experimental drugs that "showed promise" in slowing down the advance of the disease. She said I could apply to get into clinical trials where drug companies could see how I responded to new and hopefully efficacious drug therapies. A phrase from a popular song suddenly, ironically, popped into my mind: What if the cure is worse than the disease? I quickly thought, Is anything worse than this disease? Only later while breaking the news to my father would I offer-along with an ample dose of gallows humor-the wish that I'd been diagnosed with cancer instead. Maybe then, I'd stand a fighting chance.

Amyotrophic Lateral Sclerosis is a rare, progressive, degenerative and fatal disease affecting the spinal cord and brain, its onset usually occurring in middle age. Characterized by increasing and spreading muscular weakness, it methodically compromises proper functioning of the motor neurons in the brain. A.L.S. is also known by its epithet, Lou Gehrig's Disease, named after the gifted baseball player of the 1930's who was forced to retire from a storied career only to die soon after, due to the debilitating effects of the malady. Today the world famous physicist, Stephen Hawking, stricken with this illness nearly fifty years ago, occupies the rare distinction of being an anomaly in the annals of its many victims. For mysterious reasons the illness halted its ineluctable progression, sparing his life and mind but leaving him severely crippled and unable to care for himself.

But I wasn't at all conversant with the history of the illness when I received my end-of-the-road diagnosis. I felt myself spinning out of control, in free-fall. When I managed to regain some composure, I was struck with the grim realization that my son, just eight, a bright tow-headed creature, would grow up without a father. I thought of my mother who'd lost her own father to sudden death when she was also just eight years old and wondered what vacuum that must have left in her young life. Just days away from my forty-fifth birthday I'd had my whole promising life in front of me...until now.

Time seemed to speed up at an exponential rate. Everything about the room I was in...myself, the physician, the cheap framed sport prints on the wall...all of it turned into a blur of motion. I gripped the arms of my chair to gain some purchase on anything solid and tangible.

I looked at my doctor and asked her how long I had left to live. "A year, maybe two," was all she said. My first instinct, honed in innumerable real estate negotiations, was to barter away these grossly unacceptable terms of my remaining tenure for something... anything...more palatable. Reality quickly jolted me into the futility of that exercise. I began to sob uncontrollably. Was this all just a bad dream? Would I soon awaken from it and laugh at its ludicrous but thankfully unreal presence? As the doctor offered me Kleenex, something beyond even the finality of her consoling words told me it was all too depressingly real.

As I left the office I was overcome with numbness. Everything I'd come to believe about life and my anticipated journey through it crumbled. An immense broken mirror mocked me from a thousand scattered shards. Raising my son and shepherding him along the path to his life's purpose, realizing my dreams, my desires to see more of the world, growing comfortably into retirement…all of these suddenly not-to-be-lived chapters in my life now taunted me.

I drove onto the freeway to get to a lunch appointment with a friend because I didn't know what to do, where else to turn. I sought the reassurance of habit. I'd only felt this way once before when my older brother's life came to a tragic end just shy of his nineteenth birthday. When David died I'd felt a part of me had been torn out. One day he was here, the next day gone, vanished and vanquished to a place I couldn't begin to fathom. Now as the shock of "the news" coursed more fully through my being, I relived that same emptiness I'd felt so profoundly all those years before. It appeared from my gruesome diagnosis I'd all too soon be joining him in the realm of the dearly departed.

Having to face mortality is one of the greatest challenges we ever confront. Being told I was no longer in control of my life challenged my very sanity. All of the separate threads comprising the once seemingly stalwart cord of my existence began to unravel before my eyes. One year, maybe two, if the gods saw fit to grace me with a little more time. It all felt so unfair, it *was* so unfair. In the midst of my numbness I started feeling anger, resentment and rage creep into my heart.

When I returned home that evening, I told my wife the verdict. The shock on her face was quickly supplanted by a mask of fear, a fear which knew no containment. Though my doctor concurred on my getting a second opinion, deep in my heart I already knew what that answer would turn out to be. And so it was.

• • •

WE'D BEEN MARRIED for eight years. With a beautiful and precocious son, in the midst of a major ground-up house remodel, and with a thriving but demanding real estate practice to run and rental properties requiring constant oversight we were constantly racing this way and that, only sharing common ground in our unrelenting disagreements about virtually everything. After failed attempts through counseling to shore up the perennially troubled relationship there now existed only days of a relatively quiet truce...a cool near-civility...interspersed with much longer, steadily escalating periods of angry rage or icy, adamant silence. That we were already emotionally divorced was apparent. Into this unforgiving atmosphere came the deadening and intolerable news of still more upheaval.

When we sat my son down to explain the terrible truth of my diagnosis to him he was still a little boy possessed of bright, unassuming innocence. After the "talk," he was forever changed, bowed under the weight of having his world crushed by a new, foreboding knowledge. His comment to us after hearing the news, etched into my memory for all time, said it all. After hearing his mother and me explain the gruesome new element in his world he turned from his perch on the sofa, looked up at me with pleading eyes and asked, "But isn't there any good news?" His words crumpled my heart. Nothing we could say could reassure him or temper the certainty, the terrible cruelty, of my diagnosis.

My steadily deteriorating voice made the decision to retire from my business for me. My wife would take over the reins and run the operation with me coaching from the sidelines. She reluctantly set about learning what she needed to do to mantain our financial lifeline. That difficult transition took place during the summer of 1997. On my forty-sixth birthday in December of that year, while I was at home pondering my seemingly non-existent options, I answered the doorbell and was served with divorce papers. Six short but nightmarish days later I moved out of my home and into the void of being separated from all I'd known.

I remember everything about the day I left my home for the final time: the grayness in the cold winter sky couldn't come close to matching the state of my mental and emotional fugue. In the midst of deep anxiety at being forced to move away from my son, now living with a terminal diagnosis, chillingly on my own without any direction or answers, watching the business I'd spent the past almost twenty years building from scratch recede from view, with divorce papers clutched in hand, I bid a final, lonely farewell to the life I'd known.

Yet in that very moment as I drove away from all that defined my life, I felt traces of relief. It simply couldn't get much worse...other than what the disease still had in store for me. Though horrific deterioration lay in wait for me, outside the confines of a horrendously negative marriage, I had a chance at least on some basic level, to begin healing. And while I couldn't know it at the time, forsaking the vitriol of that relationship would allow me to find, embrace and adopt enormous regenerative power. Little did I know how far that would take me geographically and experientially.

I sat back in the apartment I'd rented, breathed deeply and tallied my losses: health, marriage, actively fathering and guiding my son, my business, my home, and quite possibly, any remaining vestiges of mental and emotional equilibrium. Everything I'd come to think of as defining my life was rapidly fading from view. I was stripped bare, laid out sacrificially on a perverse altar of ruin, waiting for the knockout punch that no fewer than two specialists vowed was coming...and coming very quickly. Thinking that I now faced overwhelming challenge was like the Irish glibly describing their decades long internecine conflict as "the troubles." Their euphemism seemed well-suited to what was now poised to swiftly deliver me to my own finality. It was also a quasi-humorous sanity-preserving tool to help me deal with the overwhelming maelstrom beginning to envelop me.

In that very moment of utter despair, I felt the first faint but unmistakable twinges of resolve rise up and flow through me. Something was sending me a message not to give up, to stay in the game. And although I couldn't identify its origin it was as real as my right arm. I was reminded of a card I'd received from a supportive client who, hearing the news of my forced "retirement" had written, "John, don't give up, don't ever give up." Always possessed of a strong if not stubborn will, I made this simple phrase my raison d'etre. Still reeling from the sheer weight of trauma and change but determined I would not go down without a fight I set out on an inexorable journey into the fear-laden unknown lying so ominously before me.

Hearing of my plight, my cousin materialized to offer her assistance in tracking down any potentially viable treatments for my condition. I embraced her help like a condemned man would the slimmest possibility of a reprieve.

Being a long-time student of the metaphysical, my new and willing partner-in-the-great-search was used to looking at life from a more holistic, multi-dimensional perspective than I was. My background in the business world hadn't prepared me in the least for the landscape I was entering. Always inclined to read, I began to consume everything I could get my hands on regarding alternative healing.

I read about different vitamin therapies and implemented a regimen. I studied the possible role mercury-laden silver amalgam dental fillings played in the pathogenesis of neuromuscular disease and promptly had all my old fillings replaced. As an adjunct to having the fillings removed I underwent chelation therapy where specific vitamins and minerals intravenously dripped into a vein in my arm to flush toxins out of my system. I underwent painful bee venom injections in the region surrounding my spine. I tried massage, acupuncture, Chinese herbs, and cranio-sacral therapy. I attended alternative healing lectures. I traveled to California to consult with a hands-on healer. I partook of Soul Retrieval work. Later I would take ayahuasca in a Santo Daime ritual in order to access its formidable entheogenic direction. Eventually, I even "imported" a Russian energy healer who helped me connect to the universal healing energy, to visualize "it" entering and restoring health to the source of my challenge and to teach me how to relive past lives by accessing the Akashic records. Like so many others who'd received "the news" I did every conceivable thing that came to my attention to forestall and thwart what I was being told was an absolute inevitability.

I felt the fire in my belly grow in proportion to the increasing number of modalities I entertained. In the end what kept me going were three things: the drive to survive that each of us possesses, the faith I maintained in my ability to uncover an alternative answer to my plight and the overwhelmingly deep love I felt for my son. These provided enormous strength in my darkest hours. They were the fuel feeding the flame of hope burning deep inside.

As I began to navigate these unchartered waters I was struck with how one-dimensional my life had been up to this point. Like many of my contemporaries I'd channeled my energies toward creating financial well-being. Due to the on-call nature of my chosen profession I seldom felt sufficiently distanced from my work to focus undivided attention on other things. The advent of disease forced me to drop all I'd once considered important and attend to more urgent imperatives.

In one way or another, all the newly discovered modalities I was to try would present me options for living with the disease...however briefly. What I still needed to find was the missing link that would lead to an actual cure. Everything I read, studied and *felt* hinted such a miracle was possible but so far provided me no tangible means of accessing it. Like everyone else, I'd heard anecdotal recountings of cures and had even come across verified stories of miraculous healings from afflictions like mine for which there is no known remedy. In the midst of all my research I came smack dab up against one monumental truth: A.L.S. kills and does so quickly, very quickly.

Time was my nemesis as well as my most precious possession, a paradox that startled me into grim recognition: Who did I think I was, trying...even thinking...I stood a chance of felling such a potent adversary, pitifully unarmed as I was? In the midst of my greatest, most fervent and bull-headed hopes, I couldn't overlook the overwhelming enormity of the task before me.

Having attended a meeting of others stricken with the same affliction, moderated by a condescending bible-thumping fundamentalist, I came away vowing to chart my own course through my new "challenge." Without disavowing my diagnosis, I wouldn't give it and what was said about it too much weight, too much power over me. In reacting to that insufferable proselytist I demonstrated what an "all-or-nothing" individual I'd become. My life was either black or white, obsessing in one direction or reactively flipping to its compulsive opposite.

Instead of searching out other support groups where chances were I'd locate a less self-righteous moderator, my initial experience left me cold: "Why bother with this nonsense any further?" Though my neurologist was adamantly opposed to my "doing this thing on your own...." because I didn't buy into the conventional thinking concerning the path of the disease, I exercised some much needed control over my destiny. And I opened myself up to other modalities beyond those I'd already explored.

These might at the very least help me give this illness one hell of a fight. But in looking at these potential causal links, I was still caught up in a myopic, conventional and one-dimensional way of analyzing and interpreting dis-ease. Focusing solely on external factors, I was missing the link between the body, the mind and that inchoate, numinous substance known as spirit. My real and most challenging education still lay ahead.

Like two detectives intent on solving the puzzle before us, my cousin and I continued chasing down leads. I was still partially in denial, and like so many before me, chose to believe that I...that we...could find a miracle cure somehow, somewhere. Still, I wondered if I was being self-delusional in bargaining for an escape from my death sentence. The messages all around said the same thing: "Prepare yourself to die and accept the inevitable." In both subtle and overt ways these opinions clearly told me I was crazy to think I could flee an opponent who seemed to possess all the power. Such messages came from family, friends and even strangers who, like me, were raised to view reality from the vantage point of the five senses, quantifying and qualifying all they experienced by means of a predictable process of filtering and judging that often left little room for the presence of the mysterious, the unexplainable, the miraculous. That I now chose a contrarian attitude to what had until recently been my own utter acceptance of this same formulaic, prescribed reality only indicated to them the degree of my desperation and refusal to accept my looming demise.

Looking back now I'm convinced this stubborn refusal to accept the neurologist's timetable for my demise or the well-intentioned yet terribly flawed advice of almost everyone I came in contact with during that pivotal time incontrovertibly saved my life. In my refusal to accept the consensus on when death was supposed to occur was sown the seeds of my salvation. By not buying into the conventional wisdom that family and friends almost took as gospel and zealously preached when they saw me turning away from mainstream medicine, I allowed space for the possibility...no matter how faint...of healing to seep into my life and take root.

In the beginning this was more a philosophical premise than an actual reality but it was an important first step. I really believed healing was possible. Yet in the still fresh aftershock of my diagnosis and having to deal with a contentious divorce, I had my hands full emotionally. Searching out any possible healing modality and having a willing, highly capable ally present to confide in, kept me from going off the deep end.

I wasn't prepared for the sheer loss of friends I'd once relied on. My illness created an ideal breeding ground for fear, compelling many to shy away. Such attrition was a reminder that my impending demise was just too blatant a truth for many to deal with. It took me a long time to see with any clarity the remaining group of resolute souls peopling my journey were all I really needed to count on when the going got tough. I was also, in the absence of what I considered adequate support from others, now confronted with the need of learning to love myself a lot more than I'd ever done in the past.

Over the ensuing years of my odyssey in search of a cure, as I began to face my fears, aloneness and pain it was an unlikely source that provided me with the guidance and insight I needed. What follows is an account of my fantastic journey: mystical encounters, extraordinary lessons, implausible benefactors, a saga of personal reclamation...the unprecedented story of my miracle.

2

Convergence with the Unseen

IT WAS MY cousin, Mary, who first noticed the article in a British alternative health journal about miraculous healings. They were performed through an extraordinary Brazilian trance medium who'd been working for over thirty years out of a spiritual healing center in a small dirt-poor town about an hour and a half drive from the capital of Brasilia. When I'd finished racing through the description of the many extraordinary cures attributed to this man and reread the article again and again, I knew from a place deep within my being I had to witness...and, hopefully, participate in...this phenomenon for myself.

Not an optimist in the extreme I tempered my natural enthusiasm by trying to strike a prudent balance between rational skepticism and calm inquisitiveness. Although primed and ready to believe in miracles, I'd already seen enough in the way of wild claims by contemporary snake oil salesmen touting "remarkable" cures that I'd learned in this graduate school-of-the-newly-diagnosed to first step back and dispassionately examine the facts before embarking on any new regimen. Often attractive at first glance, the smoke and mirrors cure du jour was not what I was after.

Not having experienced claims of cures of this magnitude before, I was eager and curious to have a good long look for myself. With hope and the first traces of desperation commingling in my heart, in September of 1997 I booked a series of flights and arrived in the small Brazilian town where the healer had his center. I was ill-prepared for what I was about to witness.

The Casa de Dom Inacio sits at the end of the nondescript town of Abadiania on Brazil's central, savannah-clad plateau. It's a quiet little burg busy with the industry of small shops where everyone seems to know everyone else. Tractors chug their way up the streets as often as cars, providing a diesel-fueled hint of the presence of nearby farmland. The rodoviaria, Brazil's main highway system, cleaves the town into two distinct areas commonly referred to as "this side" and "the other side." Large satellite television dishes are as prevalent as papaya trees in side yards. As in Brazil generally, smiling faces greet you at every turn.

The "Casa," as it is popularly known, consists of a series of low-slung, one-story buildings all painted a soon to be sun-faded white and pale blue. If it calls to mind any particular adjectives they would be "nondescript" and "unobtrusive." The local architecture tends to sacrifice any inclination toward showiness in favor of the utilitarian. The main building at the Casa houses an auditorium, an infirmary, an operating room and three meditation rooms. It's here where I first went to meet the healer known as Joao de Deus...John of God.

That first time in Brazil, I was part of a guided tour consisting of individuals from every age group, from all around the globe, suffering every conceivable malady. We met at a hotel in Rio de Janiero, which acted as our staging area prior to flying into Brasilia and venturing by bus to Abadiania where we would live in an inn while attending the healing work at the Casa. If misery loves company then we were a blissfully appreciative collection of souls seeking out one another to swap "war stories" about our various afflictions and how we'd come to be in this outpost so distant from the comfort of our homes and all we knew.

The following jumble of thoughts demonstrates both the confusion and the hope I felt before venturing to Brazil for the first time.

Journal entry:

Am preparing for the approaching flight to Rio de Janiero and the upcoming face-to-face meeting with Joao de Deus in Abadiana. I'm filled with many different emotions as this trip is about to unfold. A nervous excitement envelops me. I find myself swinging back and forth between the presence of hope and the possibility of redemption from my affliction to a cautious embrace of all things spiritual, unseen and ungraspable.

In an especially vivid dream several nights ago I was drafting a plan for writing a book about my experience in this journey I've become partner to since diagnosis. In the dream I "saw" the different chapters of the book materialize and was mulling over chapter names and even the title and subtitle of the book. Is this my destiny? To tell a story I need to tell, that needs to be told? I'm conscious of the catharsis doing so would represent for me as well as how it might serve as a gift to others who find themselves in crisis with no readily available answers. The notion of this is very compelling.

It may be my journey through personal pain, loss of health, dissolution of marriage and having to give up my job are all factors in the process of change that culminate in healing and renewal through the medium of words. This may be the very thing that drags me back to wellness in some strange, unknown way. It may also be a springboard toward a greater understanding of what it takes to lead the right life......something which has escaped my efforts so far.

I can only hope that if and when I come out the other side it will be with renewed focus and some new knowledge meant to help me achieve the healing I need.

That group taught me more about the resilience of the human spirit than I'd ever before witnessed. Those people demonstrated that a symbiotic coming together is the natural by-product of illness, a shared bonding that strengthens all who experience disrupted health. In that little group I discovered the almost limitless capacity for hope residing in the human spirit and the way faith informs our common struggle with adversity.

After our arrival in Abadiania we queued up early that first morning at the Casa and waited, along with hundreds of others, for the opening prayer delivered by a speaker from the main stage of the auditorium which signaled the start of the day's work. By now the collective level of anticipation emanating from all those present filled the room with a palpable energy. What would we see? Would we feel anything? Would we somehow...in some miraculous way...be cured? I felt strangely elated and *knew* from a place deep inside I'd stumbled onto something extraordinarily meaningful although I couldn't begin to put my finger on what *it* was. If someone had asked me in that moment to describe what I was *feeling* I would've just stood there with my mouth hanging open. What I could've offered was that an uncharacteristic peacefulness washed over me, odd in that this kind of tranquility was an entirely foreign sensation in my upside-down life. What I felt was a deeply calming sense experience, an utter serenity that completely enveloped me, soothing away my tension, anxiety and fear.

Whatever force was contained within those plain adobe walls exerted a powerful yet subtle influence over me. Although I felt a distinct energy vibrating all around, I couldn't identify *how* it was affecting me, nor whether it was physical in nature or something else. Far from being anxious, I felt totally at peace. Considering all this later, I would come to the realization that the sensations I'd experienced... at least those I could attach language to...could only be described as being encased by a profoundly loving power unlike anything I'd ever felt. In addition, I had the wholly unexpected feeling of returning home after a prolonged absence.

At the Casa everyone wore white in deference to the healer's wishes. As I gazed down the long line of people that snaked its way out of the main auditorium and along a covered breezeway, I flashed back to when I'd first worn a completely white outfit as a young boy participating in my first communion in the Catholic church. The symbolism was impossible to miss or dismiss. Was this déjà vu all over again as Yogi Berra's malapropism would have it? Or was I to be born again into health? The damning odds I'd been presented with screamed "NO!" Yet how had I come to find this place and what were the real reasons drawing me here? And why the powerful feeling of returning home again when I'd never been here before? I pondered these things as I stood in line anxious to discover if the purported miracles triggered by these inexplicable energies were to include my own.

Journal entry:

I've only been in Abadiania a brief time and I continue to live on the edge of anticipation. I've discovered there are seldom instant cures although they do happen. I must try and maintain faith in feeling that the whole process only begins to unfold here and now.

Once the healing channel is open it's up to each of us to take the prescribed herbs and follow the other procedures. And to implement the changes we need to make in our lives, through vigilant self-awareness, questioning our behavior...a process I've consistently disparaged. Such discipline has never been a part of my life. Growing spiritually involves a leap of faith I've never taken. Until recently I never had to rely on what is by definition uncertain. Now, everything is uncertain.

I'm discovering this process doesn't offer the benefit of maps and markers, nor clearly defined destinations. It's very difficult having to let go of control to trust in things unseen.

Although I'd been told the Casa was non-denominational, it was located in a country with a rich parochial history. The pictorial references to Jesus and Mary adorning the walls at the Casa gave literal testimony to what lay at the core of local belief but there was more to the equation. Combining other ethnic religions such as Candomble, Macumba, Umbanda, and Santo Daime, the cumulative, syncretic effect was a giant patchwork of beliefs, devotions and spiritual practices Brazilians drew on with equal fervor in their daily lives. In similar fashion, the Brazilian people have continually recreated themselves as an ever-changing culture through centuries of miscegenation. If there exists one predominant spiritual outlook it may be the practice of *Espiritismo* or Spiritism, first described by Allan Kardec in his seminal channeled works of the mid-1900's.

Spiritism is the belief in benevolent Spirit entities and their guidance and wisdom in helping us through this incarnation. It combines aspects of religion, science and philosophy into a unique social practice. Believers contend the principles and laws are based directly on the teachings of Jesus, defined and clarified by elevated Spirit entities. Their mission is to bring us His word in pure and unbiased form, unadulterated by the ulterior motives of human bias.

Brazil likely has the greatest number of Spiritists of any country in the world. Deeply rooted in the cultural identity is a fabric of belief that honors the active presence of spirits in daily life. Unlike the average North American, the typical Brazilian is raised in an environment that accepts non-physical beings as being continually present in everyday life, a universe encompassing far more than the one circumscribed by the five senses.

On the walls of the Casa I also noticed pictures, photographs and rendered likenesses of people I didn't recognize. When I asked a volunteer, I was told that the likenesses were of those who made the Casa their healing mission from the "other side." Many now discarnate spirit Entities return during the Casa's healing sessions to assist the sick who arrive there seeking amelioration. Principal among them is Saint Ignatius of Loyola, the founder of the Jesuits, for whom the Casa is named. St. Ignatius is an important historical figure in the annals of Christianity, having given up a life as a soldier in order to devote his energies to the service of mankind.

I discovered there are more than thirty-five different spirit Entities who, at one time or another, incorporate individually in the body of the trance medium, Joao Texeira de Faria, during the three days each week the Casa is open for healing sessions. When an Entity enters Joao's physical form, the medium lapses into a trance state of unconsciousness and has no recollection afterwards what has transpired. Joao becomes a host for elevated Spirit presences who use his body as a vehicle to temporarily re-enter the earth plane to transmute healing energies they bring from their spiritually pure realm into the domain of our limited and dense physical world.

Joao has devoted his entire life to serving as an intermediary between these Spirits of light and our world so that others might benefit. By some estimates through his special gift of mediumship and his selfless service...his "mission" as he commonly refers to it...spanning over fifty years millions of individuals have received healing. He is also quick to point out it isn't he who heals, only God.

The notion that beneficent Spirits not only existed but were present en masse here in these humble surroundings filled me with awe, humility and some obvious consternation, because my rational mind and conventional belief system sought ways in which to process and objectify the almost unbelievable emergence of this "new" reality. No matter all those mornings as a young boy forced to attend church, giving obeisance to a God and saints I neither understood nor felt connected to, here suddenly in this distant, dusty outpost, far removed from all that was familiar, for the very first time and in a surprisingly tangible way, these divine and beneficent spirit Entities and their energies were exceedingly real. If I doubted their presence, the visible surgeries performed on the small stage of the auditorium would soon fill me with incredulity and make a believer out of me. Prior to witnessing these for the first time, I ruminated.

Journal entry:

Being present in the healing sanctuary of the Casa is a paradox of simplicity meeting an unfathomable complexity: people from all walks of life, from every corner of the globe banded together without guile or pretense praying for their recuperation at the hands of spirits empowered by God, whose temporary physical presence is so fantastic a notion as to be ungraspable by ordinary human understanding.

Faith and hope were the oil that greased the spaces between what could be seen and what could not. Letting go and letting the

Divine force that governs the universe do its work was a responsibility each of us was asked to accept. All of us were swept along, carried forward by the awe of being in the presence of something so unknowable, magnificent and utterly compelling.

The surgeries were like nothing imaginable. The trance medium Joao, incorporating a specific spirit Entity, lifted the blouse of a woman who'd come to consult with him and was now using a surgical scalpel to slice a five or six inch long opening in her abdomen. As I watched from not more than ten feet away, I noticed something missing. The wound, though sizeable and relatively deep, exposing pink tissue and the fatty folds just below the epidermis, showed no trace of bleeding! I stared in disbelief at what my mind told me was impossible. I thought to myself, Am I seeing things? Is there something here I'm missing?

The-Entity-incorporated-in-the-medium-Joao hadn't administered any topical agent that might have retarded the bleeding. Yet, given the depth of the incision, no topical agent would've been able to stanch the flow of blood. There *absolutely should've been copious bleeding, yet there was virtually none!* In addition, the "patient" showed absolutely no signs of discomfort, pain or agony, even though no anesthetic had been used! Her face was the picture of serenity. How was this possible? Then, as suddenly as he'd entered the room, Joao-incorporating-the-Entity, having apparently concluded his work, left the small stage and disappeared through a doorway leaving me and, I suspected, many others speechless, trying to make sense out of what we'd just witnessed.

Journal entry:

This week during a session in the afternoon I opened my eyes from my meditation at the general invitation of the Entity in time to witness several operations and an outright cure.

One man approached Joao-incorporating-the-Entity very slowly on crutches. Although I couldn't tell exactly what was wrong with him it was clear by the way he slowly shuffled, his legs simply weren't functioning properly and he had no confidence in them.

The Entity ran his hands along one of the man's legs and then the other and told him he no longer needed his crutches...a comment which was met with utter disbelief by the sixty-something gentleman.

But he did as he was told and dropped the crutches into the outstretched arms of the Entity and, to his obvious astonishment, walked evenly and smoothly away from his benefactor.

When the Entity beckoned for him to walk back to him the man ambled back and without considering what had just taken place absent-mindedly through force of habit bent over to retrieve his crutches. The Entity quickly admonished him and told him he'd have no further use for them and threw them to the smooth concrete floor.

Prior to viewing this miraculous cure I'd had my own chance to consult with the spirit Entity occupying the medium Joao's form. Anticipating that meeting I'd felt disoriented as my rational mind clamored to analyze what my heart already told me was intrinsically pure and true.

Journal entry:

A door separating those of us in the auditorium from the first meditation room opened and an attendant ushered a small group of us into the hushed space. Inside stood row after row of plain wooden benches filled with ordinary people and powerful mediums alike, all sitting in total silence, eyes closed in deep meditation.

The artificial breeze stirred up by several wall-mounted fans kept the already warming space tolerably comfortable. In the half-light of the dim room a lone woman stood reciting prayers in a precise, clipped tone from a book in Portuguese.

As a counterpoint to the ordinariness of this room, the energy here was discernible and remarkable. Inside the muggy space I felt its hum envelop me and sought to comprehend its source. I learned this area was known as the first current room or "medium's" room. By design everyone was required to walk through this "spiritual cleansing" room prior to entering the "Entities" room where Joao, incorporating-a-benevolent-spirit-Entity, sits, receiving all those who *pass before him. From his perch he offers instructions and treatment for their afflictions and, often, advice in spiritual matters.*

As I watched the line work its way closer and closer to the high-backed rocking chair where the medium Joao-incorporating-an-Entity sat I observed the spirit Entity's manner of dealing with each person before him and was astounded at how little time he spent with a patient...on average devoting a mere few seconds to each individual.

Used to the notion of traditional western medicine and the accepted practice of developing a thorough patient history, his methodology appeared seriously insufficient, even curt. Often he would just briefly glance in the general direction of a patient then instruct him or her to return in the afternoon for surgery or begin taking the special energized herbs frequently used to treat physical and spiritual ailments. How did he...it...know what was wrong with the individual who stood before him? My physical eyes couldn't begin to understand what was really happening.

Only later would I learn the Entity "sees" everything about a person through the record of their lives indelibly imprinted in their aura...all quite literally in the blink of a highly evolved, spiritually appraising eye. He instantly scans their current physical problems, appraises the degree of their spiritual evolution, reviews the record of their past lives, takes note of any karmic debts and even gazes into their future.

I hadn't yet learned to differentiate between Joao, the man, and Joao-incorporating-the-Entity. What I saw was an ordinary man. But behind the façade of flesh and bone was a magnificent being of light now populating Joao's body, in no way limited by mundane human dramas, our interpretation of the world nor those of accepted "reality." Obeying laws of the universe we can't yet perceive, these evolved Spirits are empowered by God itself to grant healing we rightfully view as miraculous.

I now found myself along with my translator standing before an ordinary-looking man in his fifties with medium-length, wavy black hair and glasses, exuding an air of absolute serenity. He peered up at me and smiled briefly as my translator explained I was there for the first time. Then he told me to sit in the corrente or special energy current. That was it. My first interview with the Entity lasted no more than a brief few seconds at most. I went to where he'd instructed me to sit and meditate, to ponder all I'd experienced so far.

As I later discovered, the "current" is an integral part of all treatment at the Casa. I sat on one of the hard wooden benches laid out in row after row, closed my eyes and cleared my mind, trying to focus my intentions on asking that my terminal illness be cured.

I mimicked my fellow brothers and sisters and opened my palms upward with my arms resting on the tops of my legs in a gesture of acceptance and surrender. It was very difficult to meditate with all the thoughts racing through my mind. This, added to the piped-in music and a constant tide of the sick and infirm continually shuffling past my seat on their way to see the Entity, and the prospect of a deep, meaningful reverie soon became relegated to wishful thinking.

After fifteen or twenty minutes, a sensation slowly built in the palms of my hands. At first it felt like a subtle warmth entering my body through the natural bowl in the middle of my upturned palms. As it gradually increased in intensity I sensed it more as a feeling of energy than mere heat.

Focusing on this strange new phenomenon I marveled at the fact that I was finally at the Casa, at last doing something that while entirely out of the scope of my experience and comprehension nevertheless resonated with truth and validity from a place deep within my being. What was this energy? Where did it come from? How could it help me? One thing hadn't changed: I still possessed lots of questions but precious few answers.

Once I'd had a chance to do more research I discovered some startling facts. These same Spirit presences had originally instructed the medium Joao precisely where to build the Casa de Dom Inacio many years before. Like everything the Entities do, their advice was far from arbitrary. It seems by many informed estimates the promontory where the Casa is situated sits directly on top of a very large, very deep formation of pure quartz crystal!

Think back to those quartz crystal radio kits that were so prevalent while many of us baby boomers were growing up in the 50's and 60's. What function did that small chunk of quartz crystal in those kits serve but to act as a conductor and magnifier of energy! The Entities knew that by positioning the Casa right on top of this vast nature-made conduit, the naturally occurring energies required to augment and magnify their miraculous feats of healing in this dimension would be present, magnified to a strength sufficient for their intended purpose.

How they manipulate and utilize these energies and what the energies actually consist of is anybody's guess. The Entities aren't giving away their secret. Beyond the known conductivity of quartz crystal I sensed the presence of naturally occurring laws of the universe we haven't yet begun to imagine. Likewise, not being given ready explanations for the myriad of strange, new phenomena spurred further reliance on faith and the intuition and knowing inner voice we all possess. At the time I didn't realize I'd just entered a school of experiential teaching far beyond anything I could have ever envisioned.

The current borrows in some way from the existence of the enormously powerful and focused conductivity of the physical location underlying the Casa. In addition, through the presence of many hundreds of people, all simultaneously focusing their meditative intentions on healing, a "chain" of energy is created, with each participant both giving energy as well as receiving the combined energies generated by fellow contributors. Coincidentally, the Portuguese word for "chain" is *corrente* or current.

Although I experienced some amazing things during that first trip to the Casa it would not be until I'd returned to Brazil a second time that my prayers would begin to be answered. The following is a journal entry from that second trip, my first day back at the Casa in the presence of those who were to play such a pivotal role in my return to spiritual and physical homeostasis...my discarnate hosts.

Journal entry:

At 1:30 pm everyone began to make their way back to the Casa for the afternoon's healing meditation session. I entered through the back corridor that opens into the main hall and opened the door from this main arena room, where Joao-in-Entity conducts visible operations on a small, semi-circular raised concrete platform, and quietly entered the first current room. I took a seat here, closed my eyes and began to meditate.

The long benches become pretty uncomfortable after a while and fidgeting often counteracts one's efforts to focus.

After what seemed like an hour I felt a compelling urge to get up and leave the room...almost as if I was being summoned. Following this urge I stepped into the narrow hallway that used to lead back to the main auditorium before the spaces were expanded. I could see throngs of people gathered around the raised central platform/stage and as I found my way out into this room I noticed Joao-in-Entity performing what appeared to be abdominal surgery on a woman. There were various attendants with him on the stage as well as others...cameramen and people he seemed to be calling up to assist him in the surgeries and in suturing incisions.

I located myself about halfway down one side of the stage and positioned myself directly at the edge of the podium with an unimpeded view of all the participants. At that point Joao-in-Entity walked across the stage directly in front of me and began using a serrated steak knife to scrape the eyes of a man to my right...no more than seven or eight feet away from where I leaned on my cane.

My view was partially obscured by Joao-in-Entity's form as he bent over the man to perform the surgery. The entire procedure didn't take more than two or three minutes. The attendants then seated the man in a chair, spiritually anesthetized but otherwise tranquil and in no apparent pain in spite of what could only be called a highly invasive procedure, and carried him off to the recovery room.

At this point Joao-in-Entity turned his gaze out across the audience and scanned the masses for what couldn't have been more than ten seconds. He then turned his gaze back in the direction of *where I stood. As our eyes met it's curious how a part of me felt like averting my eyes from his intense stare while another part of me wanted to gaze deeply into those same Spirit-occupied orbs.*

Suddenly there he was...standing right in front of me. He stared directly into my eyes and reached out to me. In that moment I entered into the same Spirit-induced trance I'd witnessed in other surgeries. Though cognizant of what was taking place I felt calmly detached from the commotion generated by many observers all clamoring for a better vantage point from which to view my unfolding intervention. At this point the Entity placed his hands on the sides of my head and began to lightly massage near my eyes with his fingers. Then he ran his hands down across the front of my upper chest in a triangular pattern with the "point" of the triangle being where his fingers ended.

I felt nothing different...just that I implicitly trusted "him" and that I was very, very calm in his presence. His hands had a reassuring pressure to them and the trance-like state of anesthesia I'd entered allowed me complete recognition of what he was doing and of his loving intent but not much more. He then asked someone to help me step up onto the stage and as we stood there he said "Give me your cane...you will not be needing it any longer."

With that I was ushered into the inner current room where Joao-in-Entity sits to receive the people who wish to consult with him. I took a seat and was immediately overcome by emotion. As I rested my head on my forearm on the back of the seat in front of me I wept with relief and deep gratitude for what had just happened to me... in spite of not understanding on a conscious level what HAD happened to me. I was so filled with joy, with incredulity that Spirit had chosen me to heal, that the tears came abundantly and freely. Is this the beginning of a new lease on life for me?

Only later did I come to the realization the "urge" I'd felt while sitting in meditation in the current room had, in fact, been a direct summons to me from my Spirit hosts to come out into the auditorium in order to have my cure implemented. It was an auspicious and startling beginning to my treatments. Coincidentally, I remember that day because it fell on the date of my parents' wedding anniversary.

• • •

IT'S NATURAL TO want to understand what one is seeing and experiencing, especially when it defies everything one uses to define reality. In my initial trips to the Casa I was no different. I asked for precise clarification of the few words the Entity commonly used to reply to my always fervent and pressing questions. In my mind it felt like I was playing a kind of cat and mouse game with my temporarily "incarnate" host as I sought definitive answers to my demonstrably intense life-and-death questions...questions to which he would often smile, offer no reply but simply tell me to sit in the energy current or follow one of the other regimens commonly prescribed.

Like the steadily increasing compromise caused by the relentless neuro-muscular challenge shadowing my every move, the Entity's non-answers created yet another layer in my ever increasing mountain of frustration. It would take many years of feeling this unrelenting consternation before I'd learn the secret of moving beyond impatience and irritation into acceptance, gratitude and peace. That could only occur when faith had had sufficient time and reason to displace fear.

Besides my time spent sitting in the current I was often told to get something called a crystal bath. This involved going to one of a series of special rooms where trained attendants had you lie on simple beds. The attendant would position an apparatus with seven telescoping arms containing a long, finely faceted crystal at the end of each arm above each of my primary chakras as I lay on the bed. Each separate crystal glowed with a different colored light. My eyes would be covered with a white cloth, soft music would be played and I would spend twenty or more minutes in quiet contemplation as the differently colored light emitted by each crystal pulsed above each chakra. When I first saw one of these devices I didn't know what to think. What I discovered quickly laid to rest any notion that as odd or unusual as this machine or other protocols may have appeared at first glance, like everything else recommended to me by the Entity, they served a dynamic purpose in my healing as the following journal entry illustrates.

Journal entry:

I went before the Entity today having suffered from a progressively worsening flu the past four days. I seldom took ill but this had me flat on my back, absolutely drained of all energy and feeling worse as time progressed.

The Entity told me to have a crystal bath "agora" (which meant "now...right away") which I undertook immediately. I experienced some very odd yet not uncomfortable sensations as I lay on the small bed in the darkened, slightly stuffy room where the crystal apparatus was located.

As I lay quietly on the mattress trying to clear the chatter from my mind, a white cloth covering my eyes, I felt the congestion, the sensation of the illness itself and the concomitant fatigue being slowly drawn and pulled right out of my body. I'd never before felt anything vaguely resembling this sensation, and I eagerly watched "it" in an effort to learn something.

I felt a warm energy literally prying loose the sickness along with a slight near heat in my chest over the half hour I lay in repose. When the attendant finally came in to tell me the session was over I felt tired but rejuvenated, without any of the fatigue I'd felt before.

I again passed before the Entity in the afternoon session so he could reassess my progress, and this time he told me to sit in the operating room to receive cleansing energy. I sat there and over the course of an hour felt tremendous energy surging throughout my body...a sensation I've experienced many times before. Later that evening I was completely cured of what had been a very debilitating flu!

Not only were the symptoms gone but I felt completely reenergized, utterly like a new man. I thought to myself I'd just been washed clean of an enervating illness by a process I couldn't begin to comprehend but one I simply had to believe in because I'd just lived through it. I offered prayers of gratitude to Spirit for this extraordinary healing and for the many continued blessings I receive daily.

3

The Cord and the Chain

THE WORLD I entered, post-diagnosis, was a bold, new reality in which nothing could be taken for granted any longer. Captive to my progressing disability, every single way in which I'd interacted with the world suddenly required modification on all levels: physical, mental, emotional, and spiritual.

While I could no longer complete certain physical movements I unconsciously adopted new thought processes, surprising me when they turned up unexpectedly. In this way I became conscious of what I refered to as "cataloging," the habit of adding up numbers of random everyday things...from books on library shelves to the boards comprising the ceiling in my living room.

When I first became aware of this fixation with quantifying disparate portions of my little universe, I felt mild astonishment and perplexity. Was this fascination the result of neurological upheaval in my cerebral cortex? Or was it an innocent intruder...albeit centered in my tendency toward obsessive-compulsive behaviors...in an otherwise silent day, an obligatory mechanism for coping with too many vacuous, solitary hours, the arithmetical equivalent of talking to myself? The only verifiable truth was that I was now engaging in it, and chose to observe my participation in a process that seemed as mysterious to me as all the other events unfolding before my eyes. Believing in the power of its presence, I accepted it as a current ingredient in my passage of change. My faith in what I couldn't yet understand was a peculiarly tangible asset in a saga otherwise riddled with unknowns all coalescing to provoke doubt and uncertainty.

Still, I couldn't help wondering. Could this continual addition be a form of mental deviation meant to distance me from the oppressive presence of my ailment? Was it a salvation to maintain thought processes now often muddled by those hidden changes percolating deep within? Or was it simply the mind's way of creating order in my little corner of the universe where physical challenge made seeking structure, control and balance an instinctual imperative? I also asked myself whether it was a metaphor for transformation itself: my initiation into the halls of change after surviving the subtraction of that which no longer served my newly awakening expansion.

• • •

I RECALLED THAT in elementary school, I'd been repeatedly admonished for possessing no math skill whatsoever. The greater reality was that I simply had no learning skills at all. I'd stumbled and fumbled through class after class, enduring year after year of reprimands for my epic unteachability, just barely being passed forward to the next grade up. It became a self-fulfilling prophecy: I came to agree with the prevailing consensus by consistently displaying an abysmal lack of comprehension for anything arithmetical as well as for schoolwork in general. I was the poster boy for circle-slash-math. I'd shut down my auditory senses whenever arithmetic class began and the presiding nun charged with nurturing our growth in that class began with division tables before almost surreptitiously turning to the Holy Trinity's unfathomable perfection.

How could being asked to grasp the immutable nature of a Supreme Being help me acquire rudimentary math skills? Having schoolwork overlaid with religious force-feeding only multiplied my confusion about class assignments. Being the de facto class dunce, continually ostracized by teachers and by classmates parroting their sentiments, took on a life of its own. It taught me one important lesson: to barricade myself emotionally.

All things etheric were as thoroughly incomprehensible to me as the nuns' own teaching methods. Who I was as a young boy really had nothing to do with math. Instead of experiencing a natural curiosity to learn how life worked, I was forced to shoulder a mounting anxiety about nearly everything, from who I was to why my presence in the classroom engendered such consternation in those charged... or saddled...with my education.

I'd begun the first grade when I was five years old, due to a failed kindergarten levy that year. That failed levy prevented my gradual acclimatization to the whole notion of being taught. My parents made the practical decision to let the nuns take over babysitting me. Yet for me it just meant sliding out of the sheltered frying pan into an overtly zealous fire sizzling with religious overtones, judgment and anger. I was so lacking in any social skills and preparation that had I known what lay in wait for me I would've done almost anything to spare myself eight years of almost unrelenting pain and, often, outright humiliation.

While I seemed to be surrounded by happy, well-adjusted schoolmates these were far from happy times for me. My new boot camp came complete with its own black-and-white clad drill instructors who had the temerity to require us to attend church services each day *prior* to attending classes, an overwhelming shock to someone used to serenely shuttling back and forth between the sandbox and the clubhouse in the backyard.

I vividly recall feeling sick to my stomach nearly every single morning as I walked to grade school to attend compulsory incarceration, a.k.a. mandatory church service. Mass, as it was called, with its strange Latin incantations and odd rituals, acted as an anxiety-provoking prelude to further dread awaiting me in the classroom. As bathroom breaks during Mass were frowned upon by my duo-chromatic guards, that hour became a nightmarish exercise in trying to placate a stomach already highly agitated. To say that it did nothing for my embrace of the Catholicism my parents had chosen for me would be gross understatement.

In the climate pre-dating Vatican II, which required celebrating mass in Latin and maintaining a dogged reluctance to even acknowledge other religious viewpoints, I felt captive to a stultifying environment of doctrinal discipline. To be sure I wasn't alone in being force-fed religion, for I had many classmates...cellmates really... subjected to the same treatment. It was the utter isolation I felt as unofficial class dunce that served as the coup de grace to my already severely compromised self-esteem.

In not feeling grounded, in never having experienced the acceptance I ached for, I learned to guard my heart, to defend my feelings against the impending belittlement I knew was always close at hand. This emotional vacuum engendered a deep longing in my heart, which sent me reeling through my formative years, devoid of any purpose or meaning, utterly without even the tiniest hint of my selfhood. It was as if I were in a trance going through the motions of the school day, so numb I felt nothing.

Not only was joy absent from my typical day but merely having to tolerate another stretch of hours in that state of school-inspired anxiety pushed me to the limits of my youthful breaking point. For I knew what each new day would bring: more of the same chastisement from teachers who'd long since made up their minds about my lack of ability and who, detecting no glimmer of potential, no longer wanted to be confused by the truth of any innate promise and intelligence hidden from view.

My distress at not feeling I had a *voice* either at home or in school was so acute it forced me to make a decision: I simply shuttered my heart from the ever increasing occasions where it might be hurt any further. It was a choice I undertook out of desperation. As I would later learn, a part of my soul left me in that very moment, not to return until I successfully learned to call it back home from its place of refuge over four decades later.

That would not be the last time I'd be voiceless. In fact there was *never* a time in life where I possessed an authentic voice. I couldn't begin to fathom then the far-reaching implications of the fateful pact I made to cloister my heart from a constant barrage of pain. By closing off my vessel of feeling I created an environment at opposite to what I most required. I would feel the impact of that missing nurture across all the years still to come.

If I'd learned one lesson thus far in my young life it was this: if there wasn't going to be any support, any love, a love that truly *heard* me on a level that met my searing need for it, well, then I would take whatever solace I could gain by hiding Johnny inside himself. That's all I knew to do, the only plausible conclusion I could arrive at, coming from a mind and heart in such utter tumult. The fact that my anxieties were already in full bloom at such an early age, that I wore my heart on my sleeve, taking almost everything as a personal affront, only served to exacerbate my feelings of hopelessness and separate me from the warmth of camaraderie I so desperately longed for. It was a vicious circle from which I was powerless to escape.

• • •

I DON'T REMEMBER the point where my life first derailed. I was very young, that's all I know. One moment I felt safe and secure, trusting in the love any child desires. Then, suddenly, it was missing in action, or so I told myself. Whether it was truly absent, or my perception, the end result was the same: the sensation of profound loss. In that defining instant everything changed in my life. In the act of closing my heart, I unwittingly chose a path of pain and suffering far surpassing what I'd experienced from a marked diminishment in maternal succor. I was just five years old. Whatever conspired to make one so young draw such a tragic conclusion must have been overwhelming.

In the aftermath of that decision I grew up in an environment where virtually *everything* I thought, felt and encountered was colored by the exigency that I shield my heart from anything that might harm it further. Looking back now at those times it seems like I'm observing someone else.

Having my apparent dumbness, the ponderous, confused state of un-teachability I wallowed in, reinforced over the years of my elementary school life evinced utter resignation in me. Also reinforced were all the negative aspects of my emotionally fragile center. I accepted the situation in the same way a toddler accepts what he is told by the guiding adults in his life: as truth, as fact. My surprise at discovering the faultiness of that personal and societal assumption only occurred many years later, in a slow unfolding like the opening of some vast, intricate piece of origami where each fold revealed a feature of the true nature of my solvent intellect.

I would travel a long and uniquely painful road spanning over forty-five years before being able to step out from behind the shield I'd erected around my heart. Although disease and its accompanying pain finally brought me to a long overdue showdown with my shut-away emotions, it was the direct presence, benevolence and intercession of the spirit Entities of the Casa de Dom Inacio patiently guiding me back to the truth who were the real sponsors of my salvation. I thank them every day I draw breath.

What follows is a communication from one of my Spirit guides. That Spirits were communicating with me was as novel an experience as all the other synchronous occurrences in my often upside down world. Yet it felt completely natural that spiritual beings were speaking to me...as if I'd been involved in this sort of epiphany my entire life. I sensed they'd been biding their time, waiting patiently for my receptivity to rise to the level where their messages would be heard and taken seriously. Their timing could not have been better.

Hector* (out of respect for this Spirit's privacy I am changing his name), a Huichol Indian in his most recent previous life, arrived on the scene to share telling revelations about a much larger picture than I'd been aware of previously. As one can readily see, his language is no-nonsense, as is its initiator. He was channeled through a friend whose powerful gift of mediumship permitted an unusually clear conduit for transmission of a momentous and remarkable message.

Journal entry:

You had a strong turning point at five years old. You became quite convinced that this world wasn't safe and that you needed to armor yourself. You became quite convinced that you weren't going to get the love that you needed. So you made sure that you didn't get it. You took this out on other people throughout your life.

You need to look more clearly at the situation. Now you have a great blessing going on, boy. You've been touched with true love. You've been touched with an awakening. Things are turning. This is just the beginning. You're a very lazy man. You don't know how to discipline yourself inwardly. You spend a lot of time taking care of yourself, protecting yourself, getting the things you want. It's gone now, you can't do that anymore. You got to discipline yourself to love.

I saw a strong image of your life with your wife leaving you. I saw a strong image of that. You felt so afraid. You have no reason to be afraid. There's a whole 'nother story here... a whole 'nother story here, Johnny. You trained your mind to think a certain way but that's no good anymore.

You're receiving a lot of help from the other side, a lot of help. There are two Spirits who are gonna come...come and stay with you now. But you need to work harder, you're not working hard. You need to make it a practice to do the work that you promised to do. You were warned that life wasn't easy. You were very inspired to do this work.

There's a long cord going back a long, long time. You made a big promise, Johnny. You don't have all the time in the world no more. You gotta do your promise now. Love's the cure, that's the cure for everything, Johnny. You gotta stop telling yourself you can't get it.

There's at least a hundred Spirits standing around you with their hearts as wide open as can be, brother, waiting to help you. You got no more time for nothing but going after the heart. You gotta take this more seriously.

Okay, the work that we got done is that we got a little boy five years old. He is so fucking hurt. He didn't get what he needed. He needed it so bad and he didn't get it. And that wound got opened again and again and again and again. We're not going to protect ourselves anymore, Johnny. You gotta keep your heart open no matter what. If a hundred more people hurt you, you gotta keep it open. Keep it open to the Spirits waiting on the other side. Your dad's waiting over there...he's so fucking sorry and he can't move, he can't move. He tried to make good, he tried to make good. You know he did the best he could...you know he did. You've tried to make good.

You need to go to your heart. You need to have a practice everyday where you go to your heart. If you can't find your heart you go to your practice everyday and you pray...pray to be able to go to your heart.

Buffalo Calf Mother's going to come into you...going to be blown into your heart tonight. She's got an old teaching for you and she's gonna stand by you like a rod that doesn't fail. She's standing with the pipe and she's touching you with it...she's touching you in a sacred way. She's blowing breath into you, brother. She's got a special gift for you. You call on her every day, you need to visit the mother every day. You get down...you get down in front of your altar and you say to your mother...that you're gonna ask the mother to come.

She's gonna put her hands on your heart and put her hands in your hands. You're gonna learn how to do that, you're gonna learn how to have Spirit come and touch you, touch your hands, touch your heart, touch your feet. You're going to invoke the mother.

There's a teaching in this...you've been looking for something you ain't been getting from your family. You couldn't get. Wope's [the Lakota name for Visible Breath Mother] gonna bring it to ya. Visible Breath Mother's gonna bring this to ya, this thing that you needed.

To offer that this communication was life-altering would be to belittle the enormity of Hector's words and the message they contained. In the time it took Hector to speak from the realm of Spirit through the medium's voicebox, everything in my life found illumination in his transcendent communication. At last, long obscured segments of my struggles were cast in a new light, offering me an unprecedented perspective from which to view the forces at work in my existence. The veil cloaking truth was parted by a love and a truth so pure and insightful they took my breath away. So stunned was I at receiving Hector's gift of honesty, the remainder of the day was a blur to me. But the Spirits weren't finished with me yet.

One of the many revelations I'd discovered with Spirit guides like Hector was in my life just prior to this one I'd been a native American Lakota Sioux living near what was then Fort Bennet in the Dakota Territory in the 1840's. Notable in the pantheon of Lakota spirit protectors were Visible Breath Mother (also known as Wope) and White Buffalo Calf Mother, two very powerful spirit guides. Their re-emergence in my present life could only mean I truly did enjoy formidable help in high places, and my deep connection to that prior incarnation hadn't been diminished by time, space or the possession of a new body.

This and other revelatory glimpses into lives already lived and my soul's continuity went a long way towards supporting my newly emerging wholeness in the here and now. As I grappled with my insistent need for self-transformation, as I began growing my conscious awareness and responded to the call-to-arms created by a whole new view of what responsibilities I'd made to this life prior to entering it, I slowly began to learn how to heal.

I was also made aware that my father in this life had been an Army officer in that same prior incarnation, one of whose commands resulted in my death at the hands of the U.S. Cavalry. It wasn't difficult to connect the karmic dots and realize my father's chosen profession in the incarnation he'd just completed was seamless in terms of balancing those same karmic scales. He'd been a social worker with the Bureau of Indian Affairs responsible for overseeing the welfare of the Native American tribes in his area! I was astonished by everything being revealed to me. Yet because it *felt* right and true and resonated from a place deep within, I knew it was valid, beyond reproach and unquestionably the most important epiphany of my life, a gift of grace-filled enlightenment I simply could not squander.

When I stepped back, however, my analytical side had to question whether all these new intrigues could in some way be the contrived psycho-drama of a terminally afflicted man. Was I so wrapped up in an imagination-fueled flight from the truth of my condition that I was unable to separate fact from fiction? If so, I'd become sufficiently delusional...right down to hearing voices...to have constructed an entire mythology of characters and events to escape the reality of my prognosis. *Strange, unusual* and *far-fetched* might be suitable adjectives in describing my journey thus far but they couldn't explain away what I'd directly *experienced*. My entire sense of reality was being replaced by a much greater, much wider perspective. It was enormously exciting, deeply thought-provoking and never boring. Now there was no turning back. I'd seen, heard and felt too much to ever think of life in quite the same way again.

It took me a lot more time to fully assimilate the vital importance of Hector's message, years in fact. I'd been lazy and continued to be less than committed to the work I'd agreed to do. At the time I first received Hector's message, much of that *laziness* masked the deep fear I still harbored of the need for dramatic change in my life. I wouldn't fully own up to the truth for another four years after Hector first communicated with me. By then, Spirit had had ample opportunity to repeatedly show me the error of my self-indulgent ways.

When I finally opened my eyes and ears it was because I, too, had become so thoroughly fed up with my life, with all the pain my decisions had created for myself and for others, finally arriving at a place where I could clearly see the inviolate spiritual obligation required of me to forgive the past and mend my heart. Acknowledging this was a crucial first step. Implementing it did not come easily. After all, I'd spent my first fifty years in service to espousing a thoroughly false reality constructed on one fear after another. Ultimately, I'd be ready to embrace the truth with all of its painfully real memories and summon healing transformation. Yet that stepping off point was still a long way ahead of me.

• • •

ENTERING THE BUSINESS world in my mid-20's I found the lure of being my own boss and the siren song of fortune motivated a newfound interest in math. Up until then, working with numbers was as non-existent in my life as Latin, which the nuns had at times literally beaten into me...always of course in service to doing God's work.

Suddenly, through a burning desire to succeed and by force of will, I began to see numbers in a different light. They became friends instead of adversaries. For the first time I began to comprehend their inter-relationships, their language. As I started over again, trying to work with numbers, what had proven to be a bewildering struggle the first time math and I crossed paths gave way to a dawning realization: arithmetic was only symbolic of everything *else* I'd wrestled with during those difficult early years.

I took note of the extent to which I'd participated in the popular fiction that I wasn't exactly the sharpest knife in the drawer as far as studies were concerned. In my unvoiced desire to conform, to be accepted on any level, my complicity had been quick and consummate. My silent acceptance was tantamount to acquiescence. In addition I'd completely missed the boat where acquiring good (read: *any*) study habits was concerned. Add to that a pinch of low self-esteem and more than a dash of emotional impoverishment and what you had was a recipe for complete disconnection.

That no one stepped out of the wings to rally my cause or support my validity and potential simply as a human being struggling with his schoolwork is an indictment of an educational system that rewarded achievers with accolades while relegating non-achievers to near gulag status. My prison of neglect was defined by the preconceived attitudes about me held by one teacher after another who

— 39 —

passed on word of my unteachability to the next teacher in line. I wore this badge of shame like some scarlet letter of duncehood. It was unremitting, indelible, never allowing me the opportunity of being heard without prejudice.

Even then, my ability to *sense* was strong and proficient. And yet, to so often *sense* what others felt was a blessing as well as a curse. During those years of internment in the protective cocoon I'd spun around my heart, I experienced wrenching emotional banishment whose pain I felt deeply every day of my grade school life. I've shed my tears at how I was dealt with. And I've made peace with the horrible subjugation I experienced being lost in a rigid, unforgiving system.

With no one telling me otherwise, I *was* dumb. How could it have been any other way? The prevailing mores of the religious ideology I was told to accept often eschewed just the sort of compassion and patience for its own that on other occasions it mouthed so reverentially. I was an innocent, an unwitting participant in a vicious cycle of defeat-repeat.

I've had to do some serious forgiving of myopic teachers who assumed ignorance of a subject and/or an inability to learn was synonymous with mental incapacitation rather than symptomatic of a deeper problem. I've also had to forgive myself in having drawn myself to it in the first place, for the purpose of spiritual growth. In the end I came away with a newfound respect for the resiliency of my soul's intrepid journey and the ways in which its strength fuels my phenomenal life force.

Journal entry:

I was struck with an epiphany yesterday...when I was a boy growing up my self-esteem and self-confidence were non-existent. I came into this life possessed of an acute, all-encompassing need for love and nurture and acceptance which, in itself, isn't unusual.

I was such a sensitive little boy I took everything personally and to heart, and any off-handed comment would find its mark and cut me to the quick. I believe during these early years as I tried and failed to get love...the quantity and type of love I sought from my mom and dad...I began to withdraw into myself to protect those sacred parts of me I felt were being methodically compromised.

For me the pain of trying to talk with my folks about something so important to me and having my thoughts and feelings met with indifference or impatience (which grew out of the constant and unceasing madhouse rush that was existence in my family of origin) was very, very dispiriting. Other children might not have reacted the same way to these stimuli. Yet I did.

This abject lack of voice I experienced along with not being heard or understood eventually manifested in my need for exerting control over my environment. I remember becoming overly fastidious at some point early on and now see this as my initial attempt at creating control in my life.

Later as I observed my father's constant juggling of his salary against the pressure of more debt than income I vowed to never be in that position. Under the guise of not wanting to repeat the financial impoverishment my father continually dealt with I ultimately met my Midas vehicle in real estate and promptly began pouring myself into my new passion to the almost total exclusion of anything else.

There was no room for failure so I succeeded and succeeded further. I had the needle in my arm feeding me the illusion of power along with the guise of fame. I allowed my ego to be overwhelmed by these illusions believing I was better than I was. This marked the start of a deeper foray into falsity and the beginning of the end.

It wouldn't be until I entered college that I'd start to "find myself," blossom academically and begin to shine. By then I was playing a fast-paced game of catch-up with life, with all I hadn't learned along the way. So much had passed right by my inattentive ears. Now it drove me to success and its cater-cousin, excess, as I constantly pushed myself to strive for more and more and more. With no checks and balances in place...especially those of a spiritual persuasion...I was like a runaway train destined to run out of track. Disease, operating in perfect harmony with the duty of my spiritual path, was waiting to accommodate my highest need and purpose. The fulfillment of destiny's accounts receivable was soon to be fully upon me.

As a successful businessman I spent a lot of time thinking about that mythical day in the future when I'd finally be able to walk away from my career, to bid adieu to all the rushing around, those incessant phone calls laden with all the minutiae. I'd made some sound investments, and if my portfolio was top heavy and biased toward real estate I could see no downside over the long term. If not living for the haziness of some future date, some magical and mythical point in time where I'd miraculously be freed from the bondage of my chosen profession, I'd all but lost sight of the importance of the journey itself. Failing to heed the signs clearly posted along the way I'd become a victim of my own feverishly self-centered success. I was completely, entirely one-dimensional, forsaking long suppressed emotions and artistic predilections in the sole service of making money, oblivious to any spiritual connection.

After all I'd summarily bunched together religion, God, spirituality, and all things etheric into one giant lump of stuff about which I had absolutely no interest, given my earlier sectarian force feeding. I was adamant not to have anything further to do with the source of so much suffering. This attitude defined my all-or-nothing approach to life. Having adopted this mantra very early on I considered this way of living to be the norm, what others also did. If I took note of its imperfections during those few and far between moments when introspection crept in unannounced like an unwanted guest it was much too fleeting a glimpse of the truth. I did not see any need to change. I couldn't help crossing over into secularism after my disastrous initial experiences with religion.

As for living an examined life…without any perspective begetting discipline, I was like a rudderless ship going around and around in circles. In this self-created world in which nuanced subtleties, those fine distinctions found in the grey areas between black and white, seemed all but non-existent, my approach was simple: get ahead. I was rapidly becoming a cross between a philistine and a Babbitt: a man entirely devoid of spiritual groundedness in the myopic pursuit of material possessions. Somewhere in the deepest recesses of my heart I fostered the fearful awareness that by constantly pushing ahead, I'd have little time to look back at what lay behind me, a force poised to overtake me if I stood still for much more than a nanosecond.

Instead of confronting the problem I kept plodding forward into that ambiguous, undefinable future which though shrouded in uncertainty appeared far less terrible than what had come before. I conveniently told myself I didn't want to have the hand-to-mouth existence exhibited by my parents' constantly robbing Peter to pay Paul. It was all just a thinly veiled ruse, a contrivance used solely to mask my hurried flight from the self-created demons that had haunted me almost from the beginning.

I often searched for some memory of my original wholeness… some remaining vestige of my youth depicting the happy, carefree towhead I'd witnessed in early photographs. Delve as I might, I couldn't recall that diorama from a point so far removed from its origin. What these missing-in-action snapshots of self told me was that his…my…our pain was so complete, "we" could not endure having it brought into the light of the present moment. When I did succeed in resurrecting fragmentary glimpses of that little boy, the face I saw and the memories it evoked were of such utter sadness and confusion that I adamantly refused to walk into that pain again.

I would only return to that child's torment and the obligatory self-examination and healing he and I required through the insistence of illness, which prepared me at last to flense the source of suffering holding so tightly to old wounds. It would take me many years to confront the real source of my deepest emotional trauma and return my entire self to completeness.

In hindsight, as I considered the road I'd taken, it became increasingly clear that it had all been part of a carefully orchestrated plan meant to test my mettle and allow me certain choices within the framework of my personal destiny. This truth only became apparent to me after years spent in companionship to a disease that, paradoxically, as I deteriorated more and more physically, taught me what true wellness was comprised of and how to find it.

I did not go quietly into that good night when the message first manifested and summoned me. It was only in the precise instant when I became fed up *enough* with the lunacy of my actions, when I couldn't take it any longer, that I finally gleaned the significance contained within the core of disease's didactic presence. Its message was simple and direct: *You must open your heart and cleanse it.* And so I chose to change that which had festered inside for decades. It was my most significant conscious choice, a fervent intention I mustered because the alternative was no longer an option. Along the way as I struggled to transmute unsound behaviors, I received help...lots of help...from some very unexpected sources.

What follows is one of numerous direct communications from beyond this world. Through a friend whose mediumship allowed him to act as a receiver for messages from the Spirit realm, I received the first communication from my father who'd passed over three years earlier. As you'll see, Dad had some things he wanted to say that held special significance for my brothers and me, though my siblings were hardly prepared for his "reappearance" and had great difficulty comprehending the episode when I related it to them.

From the heightened awareness of my newly arrived at vantage point Dad's words shed fresh and important light on his personal struggles and how my own saga fit into the continuum of our family history.

Journal entry:

My father channeled through Memo*(out of respect for privacy I have used a pseudonym for the medium responsible for channeling this message):

This is my story. When I was a young boy I didn't get what I needed from my mother. And when I got married what I was looking for was what I didn't get from my mother. I also didn't get it from my father. I had a very strong idea that if I made children and if I followed a program with the children that they'd have what I didn't have. The problem was that my wife couldn't be my mother and the thought that I had in my mind for my children was erroneous.

I thought it was enough to work hard and set guidelines and discipline for my children. You know life isn't an easy thing.

Something I want to say to Johnny is this problem that you have, son, is from...it's hereditary. It's not from a closed heart, son. There's a cord and chain of this illness in our family and it was your destiny to receive it. This is one of the things I'm understanding very clearly now about family.

Families are like flowers: the seed contains what's gonna occur... whether the flower's red or yellow or blue. Family is like a tree, like a grove of trees. Our families are designed by thoughts. When we die and we leave this world we carry with us a seed of thought from our last life. This seed is a strong will, it's almost indomitable. The seed we carry in the last life will be planted in this world again.

I'm in school now. It took me some time to realize I didn't have a body and I couldn't have it back. I was very upset with this. But it's very remarkable that I do have a body even now...you can see this, can't you?

And it's true when we go to the other side...I found myself in a great hall with many other people. They were all the people from my race, the white race, that had died that day. The only thing that could come out of our mouths was the truth. And I must say most of us had never spoken the truth. This is one of the great crises that's happening to the people in the world is they're not speaking the truth.

There were beings made of light that were very tall. There was great power coming from these beings. Different beings were assigned to different people who had just passed over. The first question that the being assigned to me asked me was did I have any regrets. I wept like a baby, I wept like a baby. My life was one entire regret.

I was asked to name my happinesses and my joys. I was surprised to find that my greatest happiness and joys were my children. But I couldn't...I couldn't be with my children anymore. When I wept in that world...when you weep in this world you go to a place like a dream. It's a great hall of healing. You see the truth of every moment you've lived.

When you cross over you're so cared for, you're so attended to, there's no rush or hurry. There's no punishment, there's no anger, there's no force, there's no commands. There's just beings made of light with infinite patience and love and they're washing us clean. You fall back into this dream and you're washed clean. You're washed clean of the untruths that you spoke and lived. You're washed clean of the pain. It's such a relief to be washed clean of the pain that's in your body. You can't imagine the relief. You can't imagine the joy and the pleasure of not having a body.

Your heart is given a new...a new beginning. You see that many times you did good things and many times you experienced love and the ability to be kind. You can relax a little because there's a witness in your mind when you're on the earth and the witness is always judging. You're washed clean of this judge. I tell you a real truth: there's no judgment, there's no act of final judgment, there's no day of judgment, there's no scale to weigh your sins, there's no sins. And certainly there's no hell.

I woke up from a dream. I've been learning how to use my heart again. I've learned how to get down on my knees and pray to Jesus and he comes. He comes and his angels come and his soldiers come.

Everything's healed with my wife and my mother and my father... everything's healed for eighty generations backwards. It's a clean channel. Now I'm working on what I sent forward into the future.

The message that I have for my sons is that the seed was planted a long time ago before we were born. We were given the right family, the right set of circumstances and the right life. From the perspective that I experience now the seed is human destiny...the message I have for my sons is to examine this quality that's in the seed. Examine your own anger, your own greed, examine the quality of your own fears, examine your selfishness. There's two ways to live life: lost below the current or on the banks of the river watching it. Learn to watch yourselves.

The tragic behavior of human beings brings about misery that doesn't need to happen. You want to know what free will is...that is free will. You can live in this tragedy or you can step back and begin eradicating it. It looks so simple from this side but I understand that on the other side you're trampled by this misery, you're run over by this misery, you're brutalized by it. This is the program in the seed. There's a beautiful truth in this. Everyone on the other side gets to see this truth one day.

We live in the footprints, in the mistakes of our ancestors. We're pushed forward on the road that was set so long ago it's beyond time. We're assigned our ancestors by a great wisdom and a great machine…of hope. All of this is part of the plan, the plan is perfect, flawless. The Christ holds the plan. The plan is for every man, woman and child to one day be the Christos.

There's no mistakes in your life. Relax, don't fight, don't fight your life. Everything is contained in the seed. The day you die is contained in the seed. Who you marry is contained in the seed. Whether you have children or not is contained in the seed. Who your friends are, who your enemies are, the accidents that occur, the illnesses that occur…all of it's contained in the seed and it's utterly unavoidable. Relax.

I want to tell my sons that if there's anything they can do in this life that'll make a difference and bring them happiness it's to always speak the truth. I'm now fully aware that I didn't know…I didn't know what the truth was and I certainly didn't speak the truth. I'm not speaking about telling lies, I'm speaking about the illusion that our fear throws upon our life in front of us. This is such a falsehood.

You know when I made you boys…I say this again…I thought if I laid down a plan and a rule you'd turn out the way I wanted you to turn out like growing plants in a garden, like raising animals. I raised you like you were pets.

So I do have advice for you anyway. I suppose I'm incurable in this [he says, chuckling]. My advice is to watch how you earn your living. There's a right way and a wrong way to earn your living. See what you're casting in front of you because it's going to affect the next generation of the people in this family. You have no idea what a repercussion, what a ripple occurs from your actions for the next generation. You must weigh this carefully in your actions.

Also, I attended a course of study called "the forks in the road." I saw clearly over one hundred and seventy forks in the road in my life. There's an opportunity to exercise what you call free will and what we call obedience at these forks in the road. The tendency... the tendency is to take the wrong fork. This serves a brilliant purpose. The world of the living learns through two methods: pain and grace. The difficult fork in the road contains grace. The easy fork in the road contains pain. The path of least resistance contains pain and this is your teacher. Inside in the nucleus of pain is the great Spirit of Oneness, is the Heavenly Mother, the Queen of Heaven.

Now I must go. Don't be afraid of life. It's a very short thing. You'll have hundreds of more opportunities to live it. Don't hold back. Don't be afraid to speak your truth. I love you all. I do ask for your forgiveness as it will allow me to attend my next class...it will give me the empowerment to attend my next lessons. Your mother sends her love.

And with that he was gone almost as quickly as he'd arrived... returned again to that dimension, realm or place all of us journey to when our work in this life is complete. I was weeping at the conclusion of his extraordinary message of love, dazed by my father's unexpected return, profoundly enlightened by his insights and the purity of the truth he now lived. I've returned to these words many, many times since the defining day he spoke to me through the opened channel afforded by the medium's participation.

Today my father's gift of love continues to resonate throughout my being. His message is eternal and weighted with importance, not solely for my family but for us all. His presence that April afternoon solidified the shadow world of ether into a tangible realm, giving credence to surviving the death of our physical bodies and the permanent, immutable nature of love. That he cared enough for his children to part the veil and return to offer his insights and the truth reminded me again that ultimately those commodities of the heart are all that truly matter.

• • •

I'VE ASKED MYSELF many times, Why me? Why in the midst of terminal illness as I've watched my body lose more and more control was I so blessed to find such an extraordinary source of healing tucked away in a small town in Brazil? And why have all these fantastic and enlightening incidents materialized at precisely the right moment, escorting me closer and closer to what I've lacked my entire lifetime?

I feel consecrated by some special benediction to have been included in this mysterious process. I've repeatedly done my best to squander these divine privileges, which incriminates me as often being lazy as well as lacking self-discipline, as Hector stated. All this acts as a reminder that as a spiritual being who's chosen a human experience, I exercise free will, creating my life lessons based, as my dad offered, either in pain or in grace. My repeated attempts to hide my head in the sand were successful for a very long time. In the end, that "success" came at great personal cost. I chose a life of pain as the default option to not electing grace.

When the need to change my life became formidable enough and finally intersected with the patient, waiting truth, it shoehorned its long overdue way into my conscious awareness. I was at last ready to receive its lesson. When my stubborn resistance was sufficiently overcome, at the point where I'd tolerated enough pain and was primed for its alternative, grace was given an opportunity to enter my heart and lay down its roots. The odyssey of this physical existence I've chosen continues to involve change, meeting my fears, and toiling to become authentic and real by meeting my newly found duty to live an examined life. Illness delivered me to the doorstep of transformation. It was now up to me to pass through that portal.

As a recovering obsessive-compulsive personality I'm now thankfully conscious that striving for perfection is not what the life process is about. Embracing conscious awareness is the solution along with mending those emotions which never existed in concert with my spiritual fulfillment. No schooling I'd ever experienced was like this: an independent study move-at-your-own-pace course designed by the student, accountable to the student, graded and judged by no one but yours truly and replete with off-site mentors.

I see now how contained within my daily life are enormous changes and equally momentous lessons. What I am now, in this moment, is a bridge to my future beingness, not some dress rehearsal for an upcoming performance but the real thing. This *now* exists as a stepping stone to incessant evolution…an evolution that's been ongoing since the inception of this person I am…but which I'm just now truly beginning to see, comprehend and participate in. What I've felt from the very outset of this journey is the undeniable existence of a hope containing a powerful biological component. I feel strongly it was also a signal from Spirit urging me to open my heart.

Whatever its origin, this dynamic of hope sustained me in my darkest hours. It was biological in that it became part of my very organism, adapting to the role of protector, ennobler and enabler where through its beingness all things became possible. I came to view it as the life preserver the cosmos threw me when my hastily constructed ship started to sink. Although mapping my DNA would never turn up its presence, nevertheless it's there in my energy body, distinct and purposeful, a didactic presence I now understand on an *intuitive* level.

4

Going After the Heart

WE IN AMERICA abhor the thought of aging, what we construe as the unacceptable consequences of growing old: infirmity, disability, mortality. We don't know how to act in the presence of people compromised by circumstance, chance or accident, because honest, open communication is virtually non-existent, considered taboo by society. When confronted with someone who has an impairment excessive enough to grab our attention, we carry on like nincompoops, out of avoidance of those very fears lying at the root of our behavior.

While much of the world pays homage to its elders, we as a society would rather not be reminded that what separates us from *them* is mere time and several degrees of frailty. Instead of celebrating death as a liberating transition like other cultures do, we remain stuck in superstition; the fear of it being our turn next is an anathema so compelling it all but turns us to stone. Whether conscious of them or not, our attitudes about death govern our every thought and deed, forming a vast undercurrent of anxiety. In similar fashion such beliefs carry over to how we "see" and judge the lame.

During my yearly repeat visits to the Casa de Dom Inacio for ongoing treatments, my mode of conveyance changed along with my attitudes and beliefs. Over time, my traveling companion became a wheelchair necessitated by increasingly challenged stamina and overall muscle weakness. Although I was still able to walk short distances, either with the aid of a walker or the sturdy support of a helper and my cane, not having wheels at the ready was sheer foolishness. My new window on the world became the strike zone from knee level to navel height, offering an entirely new perspective on life's dramas and foibles. The main thing I've noticed about my surroundings from this level has, however, nothing to do with my new altitude-altered view of the physical landscape. Rather it's centered in the human condition itself, finding expression in the reactions I receive from my fellow travelers when they encounter the challenged me.

I've broken down these reactions coming from three main groups. First, are those who adhere to the mainstream-avoidance ritual. Not knowing how to react to another's challenge, this faction strategically averts its eyes or just as suddenly engages a companion in conversation that's a smidge too hurriedly contrived, shrinking away from the inbred fear we all carry of anything different, disabled, damaged. Whew! There but for the grace of God, wheel I.

Second, there's the contrived-smile-of-near-condolence. This is worse than hot oil poured on unsuspecting pates from the ramparts. While well-meaning, it carries a message of "Gosh, now you've caught me and I don't know what to do so I'm hoping this saccharine smile will get me out of a tight jam. Boy, that was close! What if I got stuck in a malfunctioning elevator with *him* and had been forced to make small talk...er, idle conversation?!" This smile is much too close to the I-have-a-gas-bubble-forming-in-my-lower-g.i. grimace and too far removed from the genuine expression of compassion it was undoubtedly intended to demonstrate.

Last of all comes the one least likely to be found. It seems reserved for that minority of the populace born with a peculiar capacity to simply be: to be comfortable in any situation, attentive to the differences, while appreciative of the similarities lurking just below the surface. Passing a person of this persuasion, I find their warm, honest glance my way is validating in its honesty, translucent in its purpose. The look says, "I don't know what it's like being in your moccasins but I respect you and the journey you've undertaken." No kow-tow here, only an openness to understand the duvet isn't the bed it covers.

There were other reminders of what separated me from the more voluble masses. When the realization I was mute dawned in people meeting me for the first time, they'd often redirect their attention to my helper as if I'd become invisible, altering the course of their comments past me, around me, even through me as if I'd ceased to exist. I marveled and wondered at what societal cue had now pronounced a judgment of deaf and invisible onto my already egregious sentence of silence. Without a ready target to bounce the echo of their monologue off, their discomfort impelled them to retreat from what felt too provocative to interact with. Instead of speaking to me in a normal manner, they assumed I couldn't hear or was mentally deficient. Once I'd learned not to take it personally, this assumptive process became fascinating to witness. As my dispassionate observer skills grew, I became a keen student of psychology and the ways in which we interpret each other.

As I changed, so did my relationships with others change. While they still looked to me for confirmation I retained my essence, my "John-ness," they were also curiously peering in at how I was being transformed by the forboding new spectacle arrogantly inveigling its way into my life. I saw how the presence of my challenge created an environment of agitation, discomfort and insecurity in many around me. I observed the ways in which some felt compelled to adopt the same feigned conciliatory facades I'd witnessed in strangers...reduced to reciting treacly bromides in the face of encountering sickness within their ranks. Through custom, habit and operating on deeply ingrained signals of acculturation, donning these masks functioned as psychic armor, protecting the wearer from both their own fears and from identifying too deeply with the phenomenon of un-wellness. Ironically, I felt my disease changing them in equal measure with how it was changing me.

These perceptions...how we see and, most importantly, judge the apparently lame, un-whole, compromised...fascinate me because I've lived in both worlds and, even now, have a toe-dragging foot still straddling each. I'm alternately six feet two inches tall as well as something approaching four and a half feet in height, depending on whether the conveyance happens to be atrophied legs or a wheelchair. My speaking voice is a feeble husk, a garbled and indistinct remnant of its capable predecessor. My legs are stiff and must appear to move like stilts when I attempt the shuffle that for me is walking: taut, unbending, ridiculously rigid in their spasticity, almost cartoon-like in their goose-stepping inflexibility. My hands are curling in at the wrists and my ten digits following suit. It's as if my body has decided that by returning to its fetal form it can find a security lacking in the world it used to freely and fluidly inhabit.

All too well I remember how I reacted to others saddled with challenge when I was whole and standing upright, existing in my former take-it-for-granted reality, populated by expectations of blissful, unceasing wellness...all created to coddle my need for permanence. All too often I so busily sped down the fast lane of life that to slow down long enough to acknowledge the presence of one so unfortunate wasn't within my comprehension. I wasn't motivated by apathy as much as the compassion I felt was colored by the resistance that fear propagates. To establish even momentary connection with the disabled was to risk an all too personal identification with infirmities that few of us wish to draw into our lives by association.

But my turn has come, arriving as destiny often does: unannounced, unanticipated, like a rogue storm. I never imagined this "thing" could happen to me. I remained intentionally unaware, purposefully unconscious that such an abominable specter might raise its ugly visage in my seemingly safe, protected corner of the universe. I did this deliberately from the vantage point of self-preservation, acclimated to such a viewpoint by the societal hush-hush where disease and death are concerned. See no evil and no evil will see you. But it arrived one day in spite of me. In a very real way I drew it to myself just as the presence of fear only attracts more fear to itself. Gazing beyond its surface manifestation I saw just how desperately I required its lesson in order to move past my self-imposed spiritual rut.

It's difficult for those not so afflicted to comprehend when I say what a profound blessing this challenge has been. Yet it has. For without it I would've been doomed to a life devoid of insight, forever skittering along the edge of my adopted unconsciousness. Encased in a dream world, I'd remain defiantly unaware, stubbornly free to pass from this life never having glimpsed truth. As is so often the case it took a calamity to finally bring me to my senses.

I am learning about compassion and empathy now. I am learning to spontaneously generate these sentiments so that having incorporated them into my being, out of a now opening heart, I can heal the long-festering emotional wounds I've carried around like a weighty backpack all these years. By healing my own life or, as another writer refers to it, my "original wound," I'm better equipped to offer the gifts of tolerance and understanding to others from the vantage point of what they really mean. You see, I now understand something more about living on both sides of the fence. Perspective is a marvelous if at times painful teacher. What other vehicle would've brought me to this necessary and much needed epiphany?

Some remarked how I seemed to have "found religion" in the process of navigating through illness. Based on my deepening immersion in the numinous and non-rational, I saw how they could arrive at such a conclusion, because in the absence of any direct experiential connection, such inexplicable phenomena can only be generalized in rational, quantifiable terms. However, the force I'd connected with in my forays to discover healing wasn't in any way religious. Instead, it stood on its own apart from comparison, outside definition, beyond understanding as a singular essence I call holy mystery. It put me in touch with remarkable insights ready to be accessed if I made the effort to understand what disease had come into existence to demonstrate.

I'm no longer confused by religion, its doctrines and tenets. What inspires me is something purer, more elemental. In deference to my father's admonition, "How's your faith, son?"...one of the last sentences he ever spoke to me...I now gladly relate my innermost truth: I'm informed solely by my direct, no middle-man-required, relationship with Spirit. Prayer is my dogma, trying to live authentically for the very first time my canon and epistle.

When I encounter others for whom my challenge causes discomfort or confrontation with their own deepest fears, I try to gaze beyond the surface to better comprehend the true source of their dread. By doing this I move beyond any inclination toward anger founded in unreasonable expectations and impatience. In its place, I try and maintain the intent of entering a realm of acceptance and peace grounded in the realization that nothing separates any of us from each other in our hopes, dreams or struggles. This is the definition of equanimity. After all, whether or not we care to admit it to ourselves we are mirrors reflecting to each other whatever remains incomplete and fragmented in our own selves.

• • •

ONE OF THE gifts that comes with being present at the Casa de Dom Inacio is witnessing both in myself and others the education that comes from discerning that, however challenged we might be in body, mind or spirit, we share a common goal in regaining homeostasis. In arriving at this realization, true mending can begin to take shape. But this must first be grounded in a framework of understanding spiritual healing. The word *spiritual* is one of those units of speech charged with heightened significance, open to broad interpretation as well as abuse of its richest definition.

What does the word *spiritual* actually mean? *Saintly, pious, sacred, religious,* and *devout* are all synonyms for the word "spiritual." But these terms, with their history of religious overtones, formulaic rules and ecclesiastical fervor, don't begin to pay sufficient homage to its definition. As I learned, spirituality is the act of delving inward, where seizing on the importance of self-awareness and conscious living are prerequisites to honoring our connection to each other and Source. It's predicated on the notion that, no matter one's particular belief, the faith evoked, or whether a physical building is accessed for worship and prayer, making cognizant choices is what is most important. Once you define spirituality for yourself in the context of your own specific lesson-laden odyssey through life, it becomes a moveable feast, providing nurture any time its transformative light is required.

Disease always arrives bearing the gift of lessons. In undertaking the work of learning those teachings, one's ability to heal accelerates through increased self-scrutiny, through surrender to the Divine and by summoning assistance from the Spirit realm...all of which I'd discovered first-hand in remarkable fashion. I became convinced it was an experience available to anyone willing to ask for relief and prepared to search for answers not limited to a solitary, one-dimensional interpretation of existence.

I discovered what binds wellness and illness isn't a common suffix but their polarity. This relationship of opposites implies one cannot exist without its counteractive other. I'd already experienced a burgeoning duality in many aspects of my journey and observed that no one thing exists in a vacuum devoid of its opposing balance. I'd watched as my doubt...deeply rooted in fear...gave way to a faith whose cardinal tenet was that its ascendancy had been *informed and defined* by passage through uncertainty. I came to view this phenomenon as elements of a greater whole, a sign of the inherent equilibrium discoverable in all things. It was this strange irony inside disease's forboding presence where I first began to discover ways in which I might heal.

Spiritual healing is the basis on which all other levels of healing take shape. It forms the foundational template to which each ensuing level of wellness binds. It's as progressive in nature as its antithesis is regressive. As I learned more about this truth, I began to see that searching outside myself for answers found in a miracle pill, some New Age treatment (neither whose terminology nor process I could understand) or buying into the prevailing consciousness of limitation were sadly mistaken as well as incomplete fragments of a doomed gestalt.

My failure to support western medicine's paradigm spared me the expectation that I'd wither away and die, following the timetable dictated by statistical life expectancy and the doctor's own inability to either fully understand or treat my disorder. Opening myself up to new ways of viewing challenge conveyed equal parts fear colliding with equal parts passionate anticipation of continuance. I sought ways in which to carve a future out of the void threatening to engulf me. Beyond the Entity's proclamation that I was being cured, there were no readily defined guarantees for me to latch onto, only the knowledge I'd create my own path and accept the outcome informed by the potent trust I maintained in my Spirit benefactors.

The more I read and the more I experienced by meditating in the current at the Casa de Dom Inacio, the greater my understanding grew: Relying on external sources for my healing wisdom didn't hold the kind of answers I really needed. Like the missing emotional nurture and love I'd felt deprived of in my childhood it...the true sustenance of love and peace...were to be found within myself. I only had to engage these parts of my inner wisdom to be shown the right path and the real truth.

Journal entry:

Last Friday I passed before Entity (after taking a crystal bath he'd advised me to have) to see what he wanted me to do next. "He" was King Solomon, one of the most highly evolved Spirits at the Casa. After passing in front of him he told me to sit in the operating room for what he called "some special spiritual work."

I sat there for a little over an hour and experienced wave upon wave of the most powerful energy I've felt in seven years of venturing to this transformative site. It began at my feet and vibrated up the entire length of my body to my crown chakra. It was so strong it got to the point where I wondered whether I could tolerate it much longer. Yet as I grew more accustomed to it and let it wash over me I discovered this special force wasn't uncomfortable or painful but just pure energy coursing throughout my body, pulsating in rhythmic succession.

Like so many other aspects of this healing odyssey, I had to gradually accustom myself to its frequency and strength before it became familiar. Another healing gift from my discarnate benefactors. I remain so very blessed.

As far as I'd come in my questing sojourn I still fought and railed against deeper levels of growth, stubbornly refusing to change my modus inoperandi. Then one day, while engaged in the most ordinary of tasks, the word *surrender* entered my consciousness, bursting open like some incandescent firework and instantly fusing to my soul. It was startling, appearing out of nowhere in a flash of hyper-consciousness, seating itself deep within my awareness, proclaiming its message and purpose. If it possessed a voice it would've been stentorian. If it issued forth as a beam of light it would've made mere effulgence seem a dull glow. It was an epiphanous event untethered to normal sense awareness operating on its own extra-sensory plane, obedient only to the implicit dictates that come with being a messenger. The word, the idea, the urgency with which the entirety of the communication materialized were as powerful a Spirit-originated phenomenon as I'd ever experienced.

I hadn't consciously requested it, nor had I been holding an intention that it appear. As if on predetermined cue, it arrived out of the ether as if sent by the numen overseeing my progress because the time had come to teach me what only it could provide. By leaving the imprint of its pressing message in my mind and heart, it succeeded in grabbing my undivided attention. Relinquishing my incessant compulsion towards control by heeding its message meant that universal love now had its long awaited invitation to enter my being. The notion of surrender appeared to me because my mind, my heart and my soul all required letting go in order to move forward.

I didn't give up or give in to my sickness but I did began taking those first baby steps towards yielding to a force that was much more powerful, divine, transcendent and perfect than that of my own pedestrian ego and will. Faith blossomed where fear once stood its ground. Faith grew into a flame of strength, powerful enough to dissipate the darkness of my formidable, alluvial doubt. As St. Ignatius of Loyola put it: "For those who believe, no words are necessary; for those who don't believe, no words are possible."

In surrendering both to the greater power of Source and to the increasing awareness that, like my many problems, obsessive-compulsive behaviors and errant ways of engaging life, so too did all my answers to these dilemmas reside within myself. In concert with the Divine, I was able to move beyond a tunnel-visioned focus centered on finding the cure for my physical body to the realization that it was *everything else about me* I needed to heal first. This would ultimately carry me to a place of lasting peace in my heart and to eventual amelioration of the flesh. Recognizing this truth and buoyed by the Entity's repeated assurances that I was healing, however slowly, removed the manic nature of my initial frantic quest. Deposited in its place was a faith-laden purpose, which centered me to fully engage in my own personal work.

Finally, I was peering inside myself lovingly for the very first time, sans judgment, absent the stultifying self-criticisms of before, now as a keen observer and active participant in my betterment. The empowerment I began to feel was extraordinary. It no longer mattered quite as much that people often didn't see John, the man, but only the disease and its effects, because now I was beginning to love, respect and understand both my body and soul sufficiently not to have to rely on external validation. I still missed it, I still longed for it, yet I no longer required my emotions to maintain the expectation it would be forthcoming. It was within this newly adopted perspective of balance where I first marked the beginning of true peace in my life.

Yet my existence still had to take its cues from the disease inasmuch as I was forced to contend with the limitations "it" imposed on me.

Journal entry:

Along the way as my symptoms have progressed I've forgotten how I used to quite literally move through each day "B.C."...Before Challenge. That part of my memory is like a wasteland of indistinct images. When I peer inward in an effort to remember how I used to live in motion in the world, I'm often met with a void that blinds me with absolute nothingness. I have an excellent memory except for this one thing. In place of the substance of recollection a disturbing fog now shrouds those actions...those movements...that once defined my life in the most ordinary of ways.

In the movie I continually attempt to replay, I can no longer locate the footage highlighting each separate and subtle motion, collectively adding up to the completed action. In bits and pieces I labor at reconstructing what simply is missing through inaction. I can describe the mechanics that comprise each movement but the film is nowhere to be found. It's as if lapsed muscle memory has also deprived my mind of its record of these movements. This is very disconcerting. I have been too long occupied with the work that disease has forced me to deal with...in the offing having forgotten how life used to be.

I rise from my bed only with assistance, only after a series of limbering motions have partially freed my muscles and ligaments from their stiff repose. I say hello to the bromeliad in my bathroom. It sprouts new leaves almost daily and beckons the life-affirming optimist at my core. As I steady my shins against the cabinet supporting the sink I'm conscious of once having turned from this most mundane of tasks, pivoting on the balls of my feet with whiplash quickness when finished. Recalling this...recalling anything from before...is a good feeling. I hang on to these few clear memories throughout the day to remind myself that as implausible as it seems, these movements can return again one day.

Somewhere inside the nucleus of this preoccupation with finding new ways of moving recalcitrant muscles I've misplaced the memory of the automatic movements that once defined existence for me. Early on my impatience at being denied ready access to movement always mixed with rage to form a volatile combustible that consumed me in waves of frustration. Now that feeling has mysteriously come to a halt. Or maybe it's just the calm before the next storm?

As I began unearthing long buried emotions I discovered more strength and a clear focus for just how deep my sizeable passions for life were. I didn't question this strength, choosing instead to believe it must spring from the resilience of my soul itself. I did observe how new evidence of this reaffirmed strength created a steadily repeating, circular energy of positive, enabling intention that fed my spirit. I still questioned my motives, purpose and ability to persevere but it was now for the right reasons. The pain was still present, only now I was listening to its message, open to how it could inform my struggle. I still doubted...as is all too clear in the journal excerpt that follows...yet suddenly there existed a counterpoint to the argument for not believing.

Journal entry:

I'm once again sitting in the energy current at the Casa. Like the constant rise and fall of a teeter-totter I'm torn between doubt and faith residing in that nebulous place where dichotomy reigns supreme. Not only have I seen no improvement in my physical condition but an obvious worsening.

I feel such profound weariness from deep within my being as if some small, fatigible voice, trying to be heard over the jangle and clamor of the disease, screams over and over again "Enough is enough, I can't go a step farther...this has all become way too much to bear." I'm left to wonder whether this journey should've been over by now, done with, either with me healed or me dead.

The disease has come creeping in on quiet cat's paws in the blue-black depths of night. It hasn't killed me in one calamitous fell swoop like a runaway bus. Instead it's content to nibble away at me in tiny, almost imperceptible but steadily compromising bites until waking one day I'm struck with the further loss of mobility in an arm or the way in which the strength has been almost mysteriously sapped from my leg. I realize in such moments, suddenly, chillingly, the relentless course disease has charted from deep within.

Am I trying too hard or not trying hard enough? What is the lesson to be learned, the singular purpose, the kernel of wisdom and truth to be found in this woe? I've long since come to the realization there is purpose in illness, a teaching. It's up to me to learn that lesson and interpret tragedy's riddle.

Hope intertwines with faith as I summon courage in each new day of promise...the promise the Entity gave me that he would cure me...a promise still espoused in my faith, however compromised it may be in a particular moment by the equally strong presence of misgiving.

I continued to confront a persistent duality in just about everything I encountered. How could I honor the strong faith I tried to maintain in the Entity's words and now in my nascent reintroduction to Source itself while simultaneously having that steadfastness annoyingly juxtaposed against a backdrop of almost equally relentless doubt? I came to the realization I was weighing this union of opposites one against the other, sorting them out, searching for that which I felt most strongly in favor of, the means through which I might find some resolution to my psyche's dilemma...if not also to my physical quandary. It would be easy to opt for faith as it promised redemption from my challenges, however uncertain the means and the timetable. Yet choosing faith obligated me to deep personal inner work if I were to truly benefit from its presence and its message...a process to which so far I'd only partially committed. Even though I'd experienced just a tiny taste of redemption I found it an appealing antidote to my old way of seeing, interacting with and being in the world.

When the word *surrender* entered my consciousness in such compelling fashion it was the intercession of Spirit leading me by the hand, guiding me back to the truth, a place I was so unfamiliar with it had all but ceased being real. That there could exist such compelling doubt in unison with the presence of resolute faith brought with it the reminder that belief wasn't supportable without understanding its diametrical opposite. In other words, whatever contradicted it also acted to better illuminate it. The continuing re-emergence of this duality offered me a choice between polar opposites as well as between two teachers: pain or grace.

Until I learned what the universe was here to teach me, the lessons would always be the same: returning on a predestined loop again and again to see if I was finally ready to learn the message they sought to impart. How I chose to learn these teachings and when was entirely up to me. While I had finite time in which to learn what I came here to learn, the universe had all the time in the world to be patient with me. If I chose not to learn in this lifetime, my coursework would be waiting for me in the next incarnation.

At this point in the evolution from out of my self-imposed coma, I'd begun considering more deeply the separate threads comprising my newly developing personal theosophy. While the religion my parents espoused and modeled for me during my formative years failed to convince me of its utility in my life, vestiges of it still resonated with my core truth. These came in the form of certain prayers that continued to echo within my soul, which I now adapted to more closely align with my new way of viewing Source.

There was no place in the religion of my upbringing for celebrating my now direct communication with benevolent spirit Entities who neither asked me to subscribe to a particular orthodoxy nor sought to convince me to adapt my beliefs to just one way of seeing Source. Nor was there room in that system of belief for the reincarnation I'd experienced and relived.

As my mystical encounters expanded to include many diverse perspectives, the notion of limiting myself to one prescribed, confined view of *actuality* was rendered obsolete, relegated to the memory of what once defined me. It was refreshing for once not being told what I should believe. Spiritism provided a more compelling framework on which to hang my beliefs. Based on my direct contact with the spirit Entities at the Casa and through my own Spirit guides, I developed an entirely new understanding of the forces at work in the universe. By revealing themselves to me in such didactic and supportive fashion I learned to *see* and *trust* in ways no earthbound circumstance had ever provided.

Through my post-diagnosis study I'd come across a host of new perspectives. They represented a convincing if not always tangible way to interpret those many realms just barely removed from our own reality. My spiritual evolution came of age parallel to the expansion of my heart's cleansing renewal into wholeness. Of course this was no accident. By now I'd become convinced that nothing that had happened to me could be construed as *accidental*. What still lay before me were continued hurdles to personal growth, requiring further grounding in peace, acceptance and letting go. The patience this evolving process asked of me was almost without end.

• • •

FRUSTRATION STEADILY INCREASED. Each task in my daily life slowly, inexorably created ongoing demands on my patience, which built in monumental proportion. I cried and screamed…as much as my muddled whisper of a voice could mimic a scream…and in that release discovered at least some momentary catharsis. Yet far deeper, below the temporary acceptance of what could not be changed but only dealt with, lurked a more sinister realization. Until I got better, until I detected visible signs of my body's return to homeostasis, I had to prepare myself for worse to come. That was the reality. The psychic toll this caused was much more telling than almost any physical manifestation the disease brought my way. Always prone to mitigate the too serious with a dash of humor, I heeded Mark Twain's sage counsel: *In certain trying circumstances, urgent circumstances, desperate circumstances, profanity furnishes a relief denied often to prayer.*

In spite of being told by the Entity I was being cured…that my cure was happening in tiny increments with each new day…I knew I had to find a way to persevere mentally and emotionally during however long it might be until I'd finally reach the other side of illness. The long-term process of being cured that I'd been granted didn't offer symptom alleviation as one of its salutary benefits. For the symptoms contained my lessons. I had to develop coping skills capable of ushering me through all the difficult times still in front of me. I was well aware this process might take years to achieve its intended result...in fact, it might take the rest of my life to accomplish. I had to prepare for whatever lay ahead. The rest was all about anticipating and managing the bumps and ruts along the way, not giving into the temptation to give up. I'd often stop and remind myself just how enormous was the mind-boggling nature and extent of the gift of continuing life I celebrated with every breath I drew. That one thought put things in their proper perspective.

I watched myself adapt to the relentless (but thankfully snail-like) advance of symptoms telling myself with each subtle new change, This is doable, I can deal with this...it ain't so bad. Like solitaire, it was a game I played to stay mentally tough while trying to discover imaginative ways to compensate for a newly challenged movement here or for a now impossible-to-perform task there. I was adamant I'd continue getting up from my tilting armchair which I was still using at the time and use my walker to slowly drag my feet across the carpet to get to the bathroom, desiring as I did to maintain as much muscle tone as possible and refusing the specter of immobility. By now I was used to an occasional fall, chalking it up to the law of averages, often rehearsing the likely trajectory of my descent and how I could land so as to minimize severe injury. Of course my subsequent tumbles were seldom textbook, never happening as I'd imagined, as if physical compromise and disequilibrium had their own interpretation of what angles of descent gravity should follow. Finally, a fall fractured two bones in my foot and I made the reluctant but necessary decision to take up residence in a battery-powered wheelchair.

About this time a medium I knew channeled one of my main Spirit guides, Hector, who recommended I participate in soul retrieval work. What follows is my journal entry after taking part in that remarkable Spirit-conducted session.

Journal entry:

I had the opportunity to have Hector, working through Memo, do my soul retrieval work today.

We sat in the clean, Spartan little home in a room devoted to Memo's spiritual work. Sun streamed in through the shuttered window and caught the faint diagonal stripe in the ochre-colored tile floor in its loud glare.

A business of flies tried to get my attention by dive bombing my head and legs. In between swatting and brushing them away I glanced up to the ceiling and saw that the tongue-and-groove wood had numerous knots laced throughout their lengths, whose designs reminded me of the abstract forms on Rorschach tests.

On a table set against one wall sat numerous spiritual icons, religious likenesses and several skin and gourd rattles as well as a small crystal. A foot-long length of the ayahuasca vine the thickness of an ankle rested in the middle of the table.

Memo explained he was going to drink some ayahuasca tea as this would allow him better conductivity in channeling his Spirit guide, Hector, a discarnate Huichol Indian, who's been Memo's primary spirit connection since dying some three years ago, and who's recently become one of my guides, too.

Shortly after drinking the tea he began to shake and shudder and make strange guttural sounds from deep in his throat. He started bouncing and prancing around the room and then began a sung incantation consisting of short and often repeated tonal sounds rapidly delivered. It sounded Native American Indian to me. During this time I was utterly fascinated, curious to witness more, yet unusually calm.

Memo lit smudge in a small clay vessel and blew it into my face and across my chest. He then took two feathers and laid them gently on my throat in a crossed pattern. Now he began an eerie whistling noise that sounded like one hawk calling to another across a great distance. He placed his lips first near my throat, then moved them to my chest and forehead.

At each point Hector...for I now realized Hector had taken over Memo's form...would make a loud sucking sound and rapidly move to the open window and spit out the etheric poison he'd extracted from that part of me. Hector continued making the high-pitched whistling sound now interspersed with a monologue, which he directed toward me in a loose and rambling manner with great conviction and truth.

He spoke of the little boy of five who'd already decided even at that young age he wasn't going to get the love he desperately needed and decided to armor his heart from the pain of ever being hurt again. That very young child...a little boy I still carried around inside of me...had to make an extremely tough decision far beyond his tender years, compelled out of the emotional despair he felt.

In that instant everything changed in my life. That choice lay the groundwork for the flight from truth and personal integrity marking the downward spiral that defined my path. In that terrible moment my soul's pre-incarnative choice in treading this path in order to learn its life lesson became my manifest spiritual destiny.

From that point onward all of my thoughts, words and deeds were focused on never allowing my unfulfilled heart to be hurt again by love's loss. In future years the pain I'd suffer at the hands of love would only serve to widen the gap between my fear-ridden heart and my inability to trust in others.

Hector now splashed water from a shallow bowl containing a small crystal onto my feet, legs and head. His first words were that my father's spirit was present and was in dire need of my forgiveness...he was in a place now where he understood the behavior he'd allowed to control his life and the way in which his choices had trained me to behave in my own life.

Hector softly stated my dad couldn't complete his work until I forgave him. But I couldn't forgive him until I forgave myself. Hearing this, tears filled my eyes and I declared a silent promise to my father and to myself that I forgave us both. That was the only way. I felt relief and a sense of vindication for the transgressions I'd perpetrated throughout life, not the least of which had been against myself. This feeling still wasn't adequate contrition for the wrongs of my journey to date. That would need to come next in fulfilling what Hector meant when he told me I needed to "do your promise now."

In the aftermath of this extraordinary session I was struck with the realization that a vast cycle of events winding far back into the past was poised with the potential to finally reach closure. The enormity of the unbroken chain of synchronous circumstances this spoke to would only dawn on me later as I dwelt deeply on the perfectly balanced order of a universe that could set such healing into motion. Most telling to me on a deeply personal level was considering how our individual actions lay the groundwork for reactions on the part of others whose lives we touch-a cosmic cause and effect so extensive it's impossible to wrap one's mind around it. I was able to see the long chain of my family's history stretching far back into time's forgotten past, and for the first time I began to comprehend that all which had come before had participated in creating who it was I'd become in my own life.

One especially telling example could be found in the first few sentences uttered by my father in his poignant message to me from beyond this life: *"When I was a young boy I didn't get what I needed from my mother. And when I got married what I was looking for was what I didn't get from my mother. I also didn't get it from my father."*

Those words could very well have been my own. I discovered in my father's upbringing, and in his truth-laden comments from beyond the veil, a confederacy of emotional deprivation astonishingly similar to my own early formed sensations of lack and unrealized nurture. Whether a product of unreasonable expectations, a symptom of parents unwilling or ill-equipped to satisfy his emotional needs or a sign of the time in which he grew up, the end result was a child who failed to receive a crucial element required for his psyche's wholeness. Lacking this crucial facet meant he was unable to offer it to me or to my siblings. I suspected it hadn't been forthcoming from his parents because they too hadn't received it in turn from their parents. And on and on, tracking backward into the long forgotten lives of our family ancestry.

Why was this discovery important? It loomed crucial because understanding its cause and existence signified that this cycle of *unintentional emotional deprivation* could now come to an end. Neither his character nor my own had achieved full consummation in the process of growing up. What we don't possess ourselves *is passed on to our progeny* as surely as what we do possess.

There was more to the story. My earliest memory of emotional disconnection stems from my relationship with my mother. While a loving, caring creature devoted in every way to her family, she was frequently overwhelmed by the sheer overabundance of work and dearth of time in which to get it all done. Gazing back through the lens of memory I see now just how frustrating her existence must have been with labors that could never really be completed, only continued. Even though my father on arriving home from his workday would enthusiastically pitch in to help her with the many daily tasks, her real oeuvre, measured as it was in laundry washed, folded and ironed, in meals prepared and in housecleaning completed, was often relentlessly stupefying...while profoundly necessary.

At some intrinsic level this was disconcerting to a woman as bright as she was. From a very early age I became keenly aware of her moods as she battled insurmountable drudgery amidst her "nest" of six sons all vying for attention. During those early years I seldom recall her happiness other than at family functions, when the festivities brought out her playful spirit and when she was truly in her element as hostess to our extended brood. In everyday life she seemed continually stressed and I could *feel* her brooding, over-whelmed frustration almost as if it had a life of its own, separate from hers, yet overshadowing her every word and gesture.

At the time I wasn't aware of my marked sensitivities to other's emotions nor did I understand I was in fact *assuming* the emotional energies of those around me, literally allowing my entire tempera-ment to be taken over by the dominating sentiment held by another person, most notably that of my mother. One of the few other times I witnessed her in a carefree mood was during the infrequent breaks she took from doing the mountains of laundry to relax a few moments while playing the old upright piano stuck in the corner of my older brother's and my bedroom. Possessed of a wonderful sense of humor she could often be heard to remark after playing a rousing tune "Oh, that makes me feel so gay." That is until a point in the 1970's when homosexuals were coming out of the closet en masse when I heard her exclaim that comment followed by the contrite qualification "Oh, I guess I can't say that anymore."

Yet at some point when I was four or five I stopped getting what I most needed from her. To be sure she still dressed me, fed me, was vigilant about my care and safety but something was now missing. Although I can't remember the precise moment when she ceased being available to me I distinctly recall the sensation...the strong *feeling*...when she and her nurture were no longer accessible as they'd once been.

As a *sensitive* unable to understand what he was undergoing, I perceived emotions even then in a heightened state of awareness, experiencing the charged quality of these impressions in a very tactile way. When the nurture I needed ceased, I followed what seemed my only recourse and burrowed inside myself, out of hurt and fear and no small amount of confusion at the apparent neglect...pun of catharsis intended.

I made the decision to prevent pain from ever touching me again by shutting my heart. It was all I knew to do. As the suspension of maternal bonding progressed over time I withdrew further and further. When I ultimately awoke to awareness I struggled to sort out my feelings and could find only deep compassion for my mother and the trying path she'd chosen.

After she ceased being available to me in ways that quenched my longing for emotional nurture, my life became a frantic and bewildering series of attempts to locate surrogates for her missing affection. I quickly learned to self-medicate with sugar. Candy offered an accessible and instant...if only temporary...gratification. Like the seductive but ephemeral comfort found in sweets, my attempts to establish friendships with other youngsters could never compensate for the enormity of my emotional indigence.

Without being aware of it, I began living a life of increasing disconnection through my contrived efforts to replace a missing part of me. By adopting obsessive traits, I sought to better manage feeling constantly out of control. I indulged in the fantasy of being master of my own little adolescent domain. Over time, constant reinforcement of these illusions only served to strengthen the guise of falsity slowly separating me from reality. Having donned the cloak of emotional abandonment my insecurities were given ample opportunity to fester in the presence of new fears. Clinging to my coping skills as if to a porous life preserver I sank deeper and deeper into the malaise of detachment from my heart.

That early withdrawal of maternal affection set the stage for *every* relationship yet to come in my life. It skewed how I viewed myself (incomplete, unlovable, flawed) and how I saw others (unable or unwilling to provide what I required most in life). Taking on behaviors incompatible with my true self, I began a slow, irrevocable spiral into dis-associative thinking and feeling, which, fostered by the company of illness, delivered me to the threshold of my present-day crisis.

Like my father, my mother, too, was unable to provide me with what she herself didn't have to give. I can only imagine her shock at losing her father when she was just eight, that it affected her in monumental ways and to a depth she may not have ever fully processed. In attempting to reconstruct what motivated her to become who she was, I examined who it is I became operating on cues from her as well as from my father. Ultimately, I held my parents blameless because I knew their love for me with certainty. Plus, I'd learned that accepting unequivocal responsibility for my own life was *the single most telling* prerequisite to deeper, more meaningful levels of self-healing.

I also knew that stockpiling my various wounds would only culminate with my trotting them out to examine, churn and lament at some later date…a process in which I wanted no further part. When arriving at the decision, the necessity, of exhuming these long repressed memories of the most pivotal relationship I'd ever enjoyed, I was finally able to restore a balance long missing from my inner child and the adult man who still protectively cradled that little boy within.

Journal entry:

I was struck with a significant realization today. All the more forcefully because in the space of a heartbeat the awareness it brought me corroborates a circle of unhealthy emotional habits that began when I was very young.

Not experiencing the love I craved so much from my own mother I attempted to control my environment and emotional landscape by manipulating external forms of power. What the frightened, little me couldn't know was true power is internal and starts at the point of loving self.

As I grew into the man I am today, I continually buried the hurt of not feeling love...ostensibly from others but really and truly from myself...under an ever-mounting pile of busyness: working long hours, slipping into the rut of drinking too much, and entering into relationships with women that were poor excuses for not wanting to be alone with thoughts and feelings that haunted me with their incessant cry for help.

Of all of the things I'd seen, felt and understood on a soul level, this was the most transformative. I was equally confident there would be more. By continuing to provide me with the safety and clarity of their presence, Spirit offered me sacred space within which I could plumb my inner reaches, tearing down the walls I'd built around my heart. Understanding that the world was exactly as I envisioned it offered fresh insight into the power of appearance versus perception. It was up to me now to complete a most important promise by fulfilling my part in the expanding narrative of my personal growth.

In the wake of this epiphany I came to the realization that my dis-ease was a literal consequence of not having *felt* my emotions. In other words, the physical materialization of having closed off my feelings found expression in muscles that refused to move. I couldn't speak because I hadn't allowed my emotions ever to be truly voiced. Bear in mind that this didn't occur overnight, nor was it merely metaphysical wordplay: metaphorical scaffolds onto which I could attach meaning to the disease in order to make some sense out of personal crisis. Not *feeling* was the actual basis for the creation of the monumental discord I was now experiencing. This gradually unfolding process spanned forty-five years, involving the accumulation of a staggering number of separate and distinct instances where not only had I refused the wise counsel of my emotional sensitivities but had literally squashed the life right out of them.

The cumulative effect of this slow but steady accretion was similar to alluvial sediment deposited at the mouth of a river as the current slows down. My pile of suppressed emotions continued to grow larger and larger until it choked off the natural flow of my most vital feelings. In turn, these closed-off feelings shut off the energies enabling sensation to flow clear and unimpeded to my muscles. I'd created an ideal climate in which grave illness might flourish. And although the disease I now experienced was, as my father proclaimed in his channeled communiqué, hereditary as well as my destiny, I'd empowered it through a lifetime of unconscious choices.

5

Living in the Hours

MY CURRENT UNIVERSE is a microcosm of the world I used to occupy. In this confined and largely homebound plot of silence, life all around me reflects the immense change wrought upon my existence... change that has come to define my predictable "new" life. From waking in the morning until retiring for the evening, I occupy a battery-powered wheelchair that readily transports me wherever I care to roll within my little domain.

In these often interminable hours I fight with myself not to succumb to the hypnotic sway of television, whose voices tempt me with and reassure me of the presence of others in my soundless trek. Sometimes I succeed and read, write and ponder for hours on end the meaning and significance of my trudge through adversity. Other days are lost to mind-numbing lethargy, a by-product of the dispossession I often feel from all which once defined my life. My silent roost taunts me with picture window views of a world encapsulated by the boundaries of my mobility. Such imprisonment insults my desire to engage the world in decisive hands-on ways of my choosing, in a manner I find meaningful, instead offering a take-it-or-leave-it, middle-finger salute to my mute objections.

Often punctuated for hours on end only by the jeering caws of the local murder of crows or a barking dog who's testy and feeling neglected, my perch tempts me with commonplace sounds, which remind me that, unlike these creatures, I no longer possess a voice, an instrument of communication. Best summed up in a reply I made to my then still young son's observation "This [my muteness] must be very frustrating for you, Dad" I said I'd probably complain a lot more...if only I could! I "talk" by using a remote keyboard connected to the television screen. Without technology I'd be incommunicado, because my unwilling fingers are incapable of forming understandable American sign language shapes. This has forced me to become a good listener...something I wasn't always accused of in the world of *before*.

In subscribing to a forced solitude, which often fills empty hours with the appearance of meaning if not its actual presence, I struggle with the constant temptation to do nothing. Any motivation I may feel on waking can rapidly turn into its opposite, a curtain swiftly descending over my interest in and pursuit of virtually everything, the once stalwart desire that had risen like a flame inside me now abruptly stillborn. I've come to appreciate that the tides of ambition coursing through me are fickle, easily deterred by caprice lying beyond my ken and control.

Within the blueness of these "why bother" moods I feel powerless to alter my disposition. If the contrary state of mind/emotion perseveres or I'm able to summon it back and rekindle its spark I often read, compelled by an old compunction to acquire "missing" knowledge, make up for lost time and prove my mettle if solely to myself. Or I write...sometimes meaningless drivel, occasionally the more elusive self-revelatory insight.

Much of my time is spent composing various instruction lists so caregivers will be aware of my needs, sans ineffectual hand signs and facial gestures that sometimes hurriedly must pass for communication. Amid this continual thinking through what will only frustrate me further if left unsaid, I ponder where I'm headed. I don't feel in the least like I'm dying, in spite of my body's overall state of challenge. Yet living in this limbo between health and total incapacitation, I find the loss of speech even more oppressive than the notion of passing from this body. Cognizant that the many challenges I face with each new day far surpass the release of transitioning to the other side, I'm put in a curious state of mind and mood: I no longer fear my death, yet I consider and weigh the true purpose behind living this way, filled as it is with frustration and battling ennui at almost every turn.

My ongoing struggle to escape the dispiriting numbness of isolation is an unwavering reminder of the barrier separating me from normal functioning. In spite of the enormous gratitude I feel for my vitalness this far and deep into such an unforgiving illness as well as for my continuing apprenticeship to Spirit, my daily rituals revolve around the tug-of-war between what self-sufficiency I still possess and the vesuvian frustration signaled by what compromises it. In the work of un-armoring my heart I'm conscious that doing so won't necessarily coincide with amelioration in my physical organism. However that's insufficient reason for continuing to ignore my long neglected emotional center. Checking my reluctance to feel my feelings is prerequisite to accepting the isolation that needs to coexist alongside a heart-opening-in-progress. I'm learning that thinking in absolutes only leaves me yearning for what simply isn't present right now. Enter the notion of *balance*: until recently a foreign element in my psyche's vocabulary. Understanding on a cognitive level that I choose my reality through thoughts and emotions I alone empower doesn't lessen the difficulty of implementing change. In spite of this I'm confident that finding my way further into this process will ultimately provide me the way out of such estrangement.

• • •

MY ODYSSEY INTO illness began with the manifestation of physical symptoms. My already ample fears ignited in the presence of new limitations on my precious mortality. In addition to my being overwhelmed by these unsubduable forces, consensus reality repeatedly implored me to resign myself to the inevitability of an imminent demise. After my diagnosis, my anxiety was more for the spectre of what lay before me...for what was being said about disease and what it would do to me. All the unknowns conspired to fuel my mind with horrific images. This bleakness threatened to rob what little remaining hope I held that what I sought to do could be accomplished.

I mourned many things, chief among them the loss of my speech. I watched as it gradually receded into memory, a non-functioning vestigial organ in the throes of devolving, even while other long silent aspects of my essential persona began to blossom in an odd dance of going and coming. It was unnerving being deprived of a mechanism so profoundly part of me, with its inflections, nuances and subtleties and one so taken for granted. Continuing my attempts at speaking far beyond any listener's capacity to parse the jumbled mess issuing forth from my mouth was symptomatic of my rabid desire to talk, crashing headlong against a reality with which I refused to make peace. I quickly learned that even exhaustively descriptive writing could not adequately replace the power of the spoken word to convey meaning. In other words, words voiced carried different weight than the same words written.

I grieved for other losses too: for my legs' increasingly challenged movements, which magnified the exertion required for each footfall to epic levels. I began to shrink noticeably as atrophy diminished muscles no longer acquainted with steady use. Fine motor function in my fingers became steadily more compromised. Using a pen to write was no longer a fluid, automatic gesture but reduced instead to a laborious, frustrating exercise as I fumbled for a way to even grasp the slender instrument. I remembered practicing calligraphy in my late teens and now, looking at the product of my focused, immoderate exertion, I was shocked and humbled. I'd built my life on the blissful avoidance of anything at odds with comfort, predictability and sameness. Now I was forced to reconsider virtually *everything*.

As I surveyed the geography of my body...the contours of its terrain now challenged by a force both of my physical form and outside its fleshy boundaries...I began to notice something novel awaken in the margins of my awareness. What I saw was the energy of my personal destiny melded to the spiritual imperative I'd lugged into this life on the shoulders of my soul. Suddenly I began to understand. I'd allowed dis-ease to mire me down causing me to focus on ridding myself of the unwanted interloper *instead* of concentrating on its deeper, hidden lessons. I felt if I could just see the larger picture, its panorama could lead me to resolution by addressing long unposed and unanswered questions.

From an early age I'd felt an uncommon vigor, not physical energy *per se* but a subtle vibration animating my creative essence. In spite of not knowing what to do and not feeling I had anyone I could turn to, I'd always sensed the strong undercurrent of purpose, however misinterpreted and ambiguous, lurking beneath my lack of direction. At the time I didn't understand this for what it was: the energy of my soul's mandate pulsing relentlessly like a second heartbeat, reminding that essential part of me still inextricably bound to the numinous that I wasn't alone, after all. It was a curious sensation in an otherwise desultory early life experience. The energy of its nearness has remained in my memory all these years.

Builders of straw bale house often insert a small glass door into one of the walls of the homes they construct. This opening allows ready visual access to the contents of the wall void. Framed either decoratively or plainly, this aperture is known as a truth window. The ability to peer inside at the undisguised contents of my head and heart and finally *want* to see my thoughts and feelings in their truest state was the culmination of intent coupled with glacial behavior modification. I was suddenly faced with what really comprised my aberrant worldview. Confronting the messy contents of the very energy of my beliefs became my quest and goal. The necessity of installing a truth window in my consciousness to expose to ready scrutiny the thoughts and emotions creating my reality became of utmost importance. If I possessed no portal through which to continuously observe my behaviors, how could I expect to change?

In returning to authenticity I learned that reconciling who I intrinsically was as a person...my selfhood...to the wonts of the world meant no longer assuming defensive postures, donning masks, sequestering my heart. It required softening my emotive core, letting go of the rigid concepts I'd carried throughout my life, and entertaining for the first time a conspiracy of deep acceptance and peace in place of the judgment and turmoil that had prevailed ever since I'd brokered my fateful pact with self so early in life. I also learned that doing so necessitated constant monitoring and vigilance, because my tendency to slide backward into spiritual recidivism was a given.

Learning to be real again wasn't such a bad thing after all. Having lived as a prisoner of my own making for so long allowed me valuable perspective as to how I wanted my future to unfold. I now had a barometer for the crucial choices I'd make, moving forward. I was then in my late 50's. If what I'd survived so far left any impression, it was that I didn't have oodles of time left to squander if I was, in the final analysis, serious about having my life mean what I now wanted it to mean. Never mind the presence of dis-ease and my continuing challenge coping with its symptoms, I now saw with utter clarity the extent of the obligation I was born to fulfill. I felt its sacredness in my heart and could no more shy away from it than halt the blood coursing through my veins.

My divagation away from true consciousness proved a prolonged odyssey. My life had become a succession of knee-jerk reactions to umpteen encounters with that pesky interloper known as *reality.* All the fallout from these constant battles was strewn across my path, creating obstacles to the delusive expectations I preferred in place of their less palatable counterparts. As I grew further in my awakening to truth, I gradually became conscious enough to dissect these chapters in my story of alienation and initiate a return to a state of greater well-being. I realized much of my laziness and lack of structure were excuses I employed for not doing the deeper work of loving myself.

By learning to cultivate deep compassion for myself and the choices I'd made and through a newfound understanding of the forces that conspired to shape my life, I overcame my habitual apprehension. I was finally learning how to feel again.

Methodically, I tugged the fears in my life into the light of scrutiny, one by one. That process did not automatically mend these distracted aspects of psyche but it did cast them in a revealing light, insistent that I examine them. I saw how fear itself possessed no weight, no real substance, save for the way I'd fleshed it into life through my thought-forms. Acquiring this knowledge helped me disrobe the dread which had ruled every facet of my life.

• • •

I'M BEGINNING TO experience what adaptive living means. In bending to meet the circumstance of disability with a knowing if not begrudging acceptance, I continue requesting spiritual insight into the nature and necessity of my journey. Yet even while people are with me, tempting my participation in dialogue I'm no longer an active party to, I often feel left out of present moment spontaneity, such is the unmistakable void left in the absence of that instrument called voice. So often, my adapting to circumstance is synonymous with reconciling myself to the disconnect that's an almost certain by-product of not being able to speak. It's both oppressive and oddly liberating, as the act of purely listening frees me to be absolutely present in the moment absent the need to constantly think about what I want to say next. In this way it becomes a form of unintentional surrender. If it weren't for having learned to endure these occasions, the frustration would've long since overwhelmed me.

It bothers me that I've grown so accustomed to being alone. The blessed gift of continuance I welcome with each new day doubles as an interminable reminder of the obligations accompanying my trial of health. My time is filled with unvarying rituals and degrees of coping that seem tangential to what I desire most: spontaneous, fun, meaningful interaction with others. I daydream the possibility of relationships, yet their potential to manifest remains opaque, refusing to become fully fleshed in the here and now because it lacks the gravitas of my convictions.

These imagined components of all-that-is-possible remain stuck in an unrealized bardo state because I don't believe *enough* in their power to become fully present in the *now* of my disability-laden world. Who has the patience to deal with one whose means of communicating is laborious at best? Just how much can you reasonably expect from those attempting to know the person lying under such an impasse? At the threshold of all that's possible, my old tapes continue to loop, oblivious to my efforts in mending thought, word, deed and feeling, intent on dispensing their fallacies of fear that question personal worth, what constitutes wholeness and how to view self. They are a less than subtle reminder that once deeply ingrained behaviors still linger in order to continue teaching their lessons.

Before conscious awareness blossomed inside me, my sense of worth was filtered through a bitterly shut heart, which obstructed me from seeing the true image of who I really was. In those days recognizing my reflection didn't mean I was witnessing anything remotely genuine in the process. Instead it was a specious argument I made to myself, a superficial act of self-deceit, nurtured by repetition, based on defending self by treating the surface as the entirety. In order to be viewed in the mirror of honest self-assessment, the truth of who I'd become required removing anything impeding clear vision, once and for all not only seeing my true image without any blinders but *willingly* with new sight.

When I began freeing my heart from limiting discord and taking steps toward self-actualization, what persisted was a separate obstacle to my burgeoning sense of wholeness. Prior to my unconscious behaviors receding my defense of self allowed a state of havoc free rein. Now that my awareness was vigilant to thoughts and feelings out of alignment with my spiritual imperative, I gradually reclaimed control of my true purpose. I watched as new intentions accelerated in momentum in every facet of my life, attracting consonant energies into being.

What remained was the impact my physical disabilities exerted on my day-to-day existence. Although a healthy sense of wholeness seemed inextricably tied to my physical travails, in fact the key to freeing myself from limiting beliefs could be found in my perceptions, in what I chose to think about my lot in life, not in the reality of what I faced physically with each new day. The answer lay in discovering practical ways to move philosophical premise into actual implementation as I taught myself a new way of being in the world. I was learning how to substitute a reality of tired, old sameness for one I intentionally thought into existence. I finally had a plan. It hinged on quite literally dreaming a new life into being.

In the meantime I came to understand aloneness was an optimal ingredient in becoming reacquainted with my center, with the self I'd all but forgotten during my decades-long unraveling. Reintroducing myself to parts of me held in lifelong abeyance if not utter avoidance took a force of will equal to the manic call-to-arms, the survival mechanism, which roared through my body with ferocity shortly after receiving my diagnosis.

I'd always been uncomfortable in the presence of solitude lasting longer than a very brief period of time. Gazing back, I now realize within such silence if I'd been listening…if I'd known how to listen…I would've heard the bells of accountability tolling. Solitude and the quiet space at my center offered something I'd never connected with before: coherence with the deepest levels of my higher self in a place where truth seamlessly dovetailed with the divine. As with many other aspects of my journey, coming to a point where I truly *wanted* to participate in this process and *feeling comfortable* doing so took a long time to achieve. It is telling how far I was willing to go to escape. I'd grown so used to fleeing the truth, the act of running away became a kind of truth in itself. It was what I knew, what I was most proficient at.

My lessons in what it meant to live here in the moment from an open, feeling, accessible heart continued, reminding me that this part of the healing equation mattered most. Aloneness came to symbolize the necessity of ongoing dialogue with my heart, in a quiet space of self-reflective silence. Here the simple act of listening could subdue the babel of noise I'd always manufactured to distance myself from any examination of the forces driving me. This did little to assuage my desire to be desired, the deep longing for personal connection I felt in my marrow, but it lent meaning where there was none before and forced me to attend to a chasm-deep need. With an open heart as my ally, fear could no longer ambush my reason for being.

Feeling again required a critical change of domiciles. I had to get out of my head and into my heart. I didn't have the slightest idea how to accomplish this, having spent almost an entire lifetime thinking, intellectualizing, rationalizing my way into an emotionally comatose state where *sentiments* were scorned as untrustworthy elements that would surely lead to trouble if given time to fester. As I was to learn, moving out of the dutiful security of the analyzing mind into the terra incognita governed by heart didn't mean loss of the use of my mind. It meant gaining proficiency in seeing, feeling and thinking *through* my heart by replacing my uni-dimensional perspective with one much more multi-faceted. By funneling all my senses and my thoughts through the seat of love and compassion, I could reclaim all that was interrupted by my early decision to hide behind the veil of fear.

I spent many, many years reactively acting out unconscious behaviors in every aspect of my existence. A notable miracle... among many...is that I was able to escape my prison and shrug off my blinders. My most enduring challenge remains bringing conscious awareness to bear on my as yet inadequately trained thoughts and emotions. I visualize my still lingering "carry-over" thoughts and emotions as a field of stumps. As I unearth the roots of one stump and then another, I effectively clear away old patterns and beliefs that don't support newly clarified intentions. This ongoing effort requires a discipline which ebbs or flows subject to caprice, frustration and indolence in any given day. It remains some of my most profound inner work.

I realize that during this process of deep healing I'll still feel the aloneness press in on me. It isn't loneliness itself, nor is it utter despair centered in depression, just the dull, numbing presence of how solitary the nature of this voiceless journey can often be. In spite of my small circle of caregivers, an occasional visit from a friend or family member, I exist in a space curiously unreal, drawn in on itself like some curled-up fetal dream. My attempts to describe what it's like to live in these margins feel ineffectual. I want those interested in me and my forced odyssey to comprehend my true pain and suffering, to fathom who I've become. Yet I myself don't know who it is I've morphed into through my captivity to challenge. After endeavoring to describe what I'm experiencing in language others are in no way able to understand, I find it's more often an exercise in futility than in illumination. I've learned to try and let go of the compelling need to explain and, instead, to simply be and see where it leads me.

In this indescribable spot I'm often struck by the recurring sense that I'm waiting for either death or life to exert the upper hand, to lead me closer to my truest self, my greatest teaching. Will I soon return to Spirit from this body or, cured of affliction, become a wounded healer, returning from the brink with some transformative, curative truth meant to help others deal with and overcome their own struggles?

Journal entry:

Along my route through mounting physical challenge, illness continues to break me, tearing me down to almost nothing, to a point where my progressive alteration into a kind of non-existence is itself becoming concrete...more real than reality.

It hasn't happened all at once, instead in frequent sorties spread out over many years of captivity to a state of mind which denies even while it illuminates.

In this landscape of continuous assaults on my well-being I often feel all that remains of my once resilient façade is the essence of my spirit, itself stretched to the breaking point...now weak, wobbly and disoriented...more a memory of what once was than a vital substance capable of continuance.

When you are broken down in this way you can turn in one of two directions. You can recoil into a place inside yourself reserved for hiding from unspeakable traumas...a place that soothes you with false, deadly warmth like you feel when hypothermic. Or you can make the choice to latch onto those remaining threads of strength at your very core and hang on for dear life. I choose...at least for now... to hang on, fearful that if I don't I'll risk losing what tenuous grasp I have on my remaining sanity...and life.

At the bottom the pain is so great, so complete, it surrounds you with its fury, consuming any attempt at making sense out of your plight. You exist in a space so confined it could just as well be a tunnel. Time stops registering its passage as you move from one jarring ambush to the next, connected to your self only by the utter fatigue you feel in your soul. That place...this place...is a hell. And by passing through these flames, everything is burnt away, all is cleansed whether you want it cleansed or not, for you are not the one in charge.

In this place you become a lightning rod for transformation. Pain informs you, becomes your teacher, drawing to you all that cannot be learned outside the gates of agony. This rite of passage allows matriculation to a new plane of awareness that's both humbling and enabling. If, that is, you can somehow muster what it takes to make it that far.

Conventional wisdom masquerading as western medicine long ago said its goodbyes to me and my inane dreams of soldiering on. The Entity told me something altogether different fostering hope where there had been at most a meager supply. I've opted to follow instructions and guidance emanating from an unseen realm that, though not fully comprehensible by any rational standard, has already proven its assistive intent. While I've come to trust implicitly what issues from this extraordinary sphere, I've learned there won't necessarily be additional answers. The decision I made lies outside rational thought as it must. It springs from hope and from a faith resiliently deep within my heart, profoundly informed by a resonating truth vibrating at my center. It harkens from where intuition and trust intersect.

Dealing with whatever lies in front of me is made easier with the knowledge that though I may often feel like a recluse, I am never really alone. Facing up to my past has given me courage to face the future.

• • •

MY GREY MATTER has changed. My ability to multi-task, to process data, emotions, even noise, is affected by alterations, I suspect, in my brain chemistry, brought on by the illness. My moods sometimes swing on an erratic, unpredictable pendulum not within my control. Like some modern day Democritus I often laugh totally out of control at situations completely devoid of humorous context, my ability to moderate such responses gone haywire by a mysterious switch deep inside my head frequently stuck in the "on" position. Neurologists call this condition pseudo-bulbar palsy, an odd aside to the dis-ease that infiltrated my being. When these risible moments arrive, I try and bite my lip in a last ditch effort to thwart the gut-wrenching belly laughs I know will hurt, wracking my body with spasming muscles. One neurologist wryly observed that, considering the errant "switch" could've been flipped to the cry mode instead of its more affable counterpart, "laughing is the lesser of two evils."

A few intrepid souls suitably schooled in my garbled patois actually understand about half of what I try and say through a patient process involving equal parts intent listening, educated guesswork, plus a dash of intuitive knowing. These days, though, it's seldom worth the enormous expenditure of energy to try and force semi-comprehensible sounds out of my mouth when they can still be pointed to on my small alphabet board or written on the tv screen that's connected to my computer. A now deceased friend of mine, stricken with the same affliction, said it well...if not haltingly: "It feels like I have a piano on my tongue when I try and talk." "Upright or grand?" I would've responded...if only I could've.

I imagine myself as a pair of beach sandals flip-flopping between entering the day with purpose and determination or without any motivation whatsoever. Accepting this dichotomy is one in a long string of adjustments in the landscape of challenge to which surrender often seems non-negotiable. I don't like not being in control, incapable of managing more than gross, jerky physical movements, which are Frankenstein-like in their lack of pliancy. Anger, resentment and near rage keep close company with gratitude, awe and the cognizance of continued blessings in this singular space where opposites seem intent on confusing me with their disparate, dualistic, yet oddly similar messages.

I keep hearing the Entity's words, "You will walk again on your own" ping-pong through my mind, tempting me with the promise that this nightmare will be over some day. With each new day I gaze in the mirror, searching for even the tiniest sign that things are turning the corner on the road to recovery. And although my condition has largely plateaued over the course of the past four or five years, it hasn't yet improved in a discernible way that's sufficient cause to go out and buy a pair of running shoes.

Stepping back from the new worldview I embraced as I adapted to challenge, I see how fantastic, how sensational my story must seem to those who hear my claims of receiving help from another realm. In some ways, even though I've lived in the middle of transcendent phenomena for many years, I still have to stop and pinch myself to make sure I'm not dreaming. If I hadn't heard the Entity's words and seen the trance medium incorporating the Entity as it operated on numerous people I wouldn't believe such extraordinary statements myself. Yet, once I'd experienced the direct, tangible presence of Spirit...not once but hundreds of times...my way of viewing this world and non-ordinary reality changed forever.

Journal entry:

This afternoon's session at the Casa was an effective time of prayer, invoking Spirit and asking for guidance. By focusing on my breathing and finding the stillness within I connected with the Casa's energies and felt the strong, sustained current enter through my palms.

I asked the Entities to use my connection to the current to assist those less fortunate, so my ability to conduct the healing energy could be focused to help others. I'm finally beginning to understand the benefits of giving instead of always asking, asking, asking. I know in my heart I receive exactly what I need so why bother coming from a place where need is presumed to exist?

I've also started again invoking two very special Spirit helpers who my discarnate Huichol Indian Spirit guide first introduced me to two years ago. They are powerful, historically significant Lakota Indian Spirit figures...White Buffalo Calf Mother and Visible Breath Mother. They are enduring vestiges from my previous life as a Lakota. They further connect me to that part of myself bridging the past into this life's journey. I invoke their presence to learn how to open my heart and what giving and receiving love really mean.

Writing about this now I confess it reads like a story about someone else, another person far removed from my world. Yet it isn't. These are all part of my extraordinary journey. The strange thing is I completely accept them as a natural consequence of having discovered this sacred place where Spirits are real presences manipulating enormous healing powers. It's become more of a graspable reality than the reality I stepped out of when I took the leap of faith and ventured here to the Casa de Dom Inacio.

The synchronicities here are often so sharply focused, clearly detailed like a well drawn map showing you what to look for. I don't mean finding answers is any easier here. But the feeling I get...and it is beyond intuitive and much more clairsentient...now when I meet someone I "know" whether or not that seemingly chance encounter is predestined.

There seems to be a clarity here I don't experience elsewhere, quite possibly that I can't experience, certainly not back home in the States in ordinary, everyday waking consciousness. Among other things that speaks to the enormous spiritual energies present here.

Losing control makes me want even more control over what I'm still able to direct in life. After all, control is emblematic of who I was and the way I lived for forty-five years. Its illusion of power led me to believe I could insure unrelenting influence over the forces conspiring to uncover my deepest secrets. Maintaining dominance over circumstance and a tight rein on emotion lent me the air of invincibility I required. I couldn't perceive that what I most needed wasn't further distancing myself from truth but drawing it closer to my heart through invocation.

In spite of my best attempts, I feel myself at the deepest levels becoming more subservient to disease's wrath. I'm struck with the thought that it's often enough to simply make it through another day, that I don't need to constantly do battle against this *presence*, laboring under the illusion that by accomplishing more I'll somehow be able to thwart its power over me. True to my reactive temperament, for a long time this was my response to the stimulus evoked by illness. It...illness...is in many ways a twin to me: a partner in a forboding dance, a conspirator in a process set into motion long before I entered this life and this body.

• • •

WHEN DEPRESSION FINALLY appeared, it washed over me with enormous, debilitating ferocity. Although aware of it lurking at the edge of my emotions, I was unprepared for the sheer power it exerted over every aspect of my existence. I was caught in the eye of a storm, my mind fully cognizant inside a curious calm while all around me the detritus whipped up by its wrath cascaded this way and that. A torrent of blueness flooded my every motion with its incapacitating torpor, reducing even the basic joys of eating or going on an otherwise fun outing into an experience devoid of life's celebratory verve. Inside this cocoon of joylessness, I was conscious enough to realize I was being given rare and objective access to a gift of insight no less powerful than this very *thing* that threatened to swallow me whole.

I marveled at my ability to hold two such divergent perspectives simultaneously: the beast of depression gnawing away at my emotions all the while feeling illuminated by the reviving spark of melancholy's antonym. Yet reliance on the left brain's rationale wasn't adequate to halt being anesthetized by this great oppressive blue wave in the midst of whose physical intensity nothing mattered. Joy scurried away with the same terrible speed with which gloom first entered. Adrift on a tide of unremitting languor I gave up and gave in to the narcotizing dejection, out of abject fatigue more than anything else.

I'd been fighting such a long time. With literally each footstep I exerted my willpower in double and triple measure to each challenged or unresponsive motion of my limbs, just to coax them a bit further. Now the only reward for all my effort was this furrow of despair and the realization I'd become the vanquished, prostrating himself before the victor. Once more I wondered if giving in was the same thing as giving up, whether "fighting the good fight" meant *enough* to try and carry on a bit longer. These thoughts were the disquieting semantics of an obstinate man not yet ready to face his own mounting frailty...if not his very mortality.

During this emotionally turbulent time I was shown how to do shamanic journeying. Like so many other doors opening to me, it was a profound revelation, arriving at the nadir of my odyssey. What follows is a record of my first shamanic journey taken to the upper world where my guides awaited me with transformative insights.

Journal entry:

I began my first journey at a tidal pool near a cabin on the Washington coast where I used to vacation with my family as a child. This was a place where I'd always felt a certain magic, where I remember feeling for the first time being in the presence of a remarkable energy.

I'd chosen this place as the "stepping off" point in my first journey and in subsequent ones, due to the vibrant energy I'd always experienced there. At the time I had no way of comprehending what this energy was. Later I would come to understand that the powerful energies I'd connected with while spending time there as an adolescent were due to the long history of Native American involvement in the immediate vicinity...a fact which supported my previous life connection with these same tribal energies even in present day.

I quieted my mind and slowly relaxed myself. I first pictured what I was about to do. In my mind's eye I then entered the shallow pool, lay down on my back in the sun-warmed saltwater and as the drum beats grew louder was taken up in the air by a powerful waterspout. Eventually I broke through a layer of clouds and began "broadcasting" my fervent intent to meet my Spirit guide.

After a while a being....a man...with a long beard and dressed in a robe approached me. I asked him if he was my Spirit guide. He replied that he wasn't. When I asked him if he'd take me to my Spirit guide he said he would. This is when I recognized him as King Solomon.

We began walking along a road with columns on either side and came to a city of tall glass-like structures. Once I'd looked more closely at these buildings, I realized I could see all of the way through them. After searching for awhile we came across a very tall being without a discernible face who was clothed in a shiny, almost metallic light. I asked him if he was my Spirit guide and he replied he was. He told me he was Stephen, that he was a being of light, had never incorporated into physical form, and had always been my guide.

I remember asking him a series of rapid-fire questions: Could he help me with my illness? (Yes, he was already doing so, and the work undertaken by the Entities at the Casa de Dom Inacio was vital in my healing.) Could he help me find my true purpose for being in this life? (Yes, following my soul's work here was very important.)

We then entered an almost philosophical discussion about my creative expression and about the many choices I had in life. He explained that my illness was carried over from another existence so I might learn some further soul lessons here in this incarnation. I asked him...Do you mean about patience and faith (as the Entity has reminded me of many times)? His response was that these were among my important lessons.

I also questioned him over and over again if what I was experiencing in "being" there wasn't just a product of my imagination. He told me my imagination was real and there was no separation between it and my comprehension of reality, that each existed as a consequence of my thoughtforms. He stated over and over again he was always available to me and would always guide me. All I needed to do was summon him.

After walking some time further we came across a pool of water where I noticed enormous purple water lilies floating on the surface. When I looked more closely I saw fully grown men lying in them... one man to each plant...in a semi-fetal position, unclothed, not moving, not speaking and not turned in such a way that I could see their faces.

Stephen offered no comments at this pool. I was so engrossed in observing this new phenomenon I didn't think to ask him about it. A moment later I knew instinctively these were mini-prisons out of which these men needed to escape in order to become whole again.

What seemed odd was there was virtually nothing impeding them from pushing on the soft, green plant wall and escaping, except the unmistakable presence of fear which seemed so great it prevented them from seeing their predicament was easily resolvable. I instinctively knew in this moment that this scene was a visual lesson for me to more fully love myself by letting go of fear.

Then I heard the drum signal calling me back from my journey and easily returned to the tidal pool.

By this point I'd experienced repeated "conversations" with a variety of beings not possessed of physical bodies. The cumulative effect of all this dialogue was that it was apparent I'd discovered a whole new manner of interpreting reality. That *reality* was actually a generalized term encompassing myriad levels of consciousness, countless dimensions of existence and infinite forms of life. What's more, I began to see how answers to my most profound questions could be *readily* accessed in realms of consciousness far less confining than those laboring within the constraints of the consensus paradigm.

What struck me most in all this were two things: how easily I was able to access these separate yet complimentary dimensions and how natural and true it felt, resonating within my deepest core. I was sufficiently deep into my journey of insight to realize these communications were invaluable components in my healing as well as extraordinary gifts catapulting my awareness beyond anything I could've dreamt. Now there was no turning back, even if I'd had the desire to devolve into my before-ness.

And all the while the extraordinary continued unfolding right in front of me. I vividly remember one especially riveting example of this numinous attunement while I was seated in meditation in the current at the Casa. It was the final day of a trip to that blessed, sacred site.

Journal entry:

I opened my work of meditation in the current by invoking the presence and guidance of Saint Ignatius to whom I've developed an increasing closeness during this stay. I've prayed to him on a number of occasions and always received a response in one form or another.

While my chief Spirit physician is Dr. Algosto de Almeida I don't feel quite the same connection to him as I do with St. Ignatius, as the former's manner is often brusque and business-like while the latter is known for his extraordinary patience, kindness and loving style.

The energy and my connection to the current began slowly then steadily grew in intensity throughout the first two hours of the three-hour meditation. During this time I felt an influx of energy radiating up my forearms from its entry point in my palms.

At about two hours into the work I suddenly felt a sensation in my heart as if someone was poking me with a sharp object deep inside that organ. It didn't resemble any feeling I'd ever had. While it was a sharp near-pain, I didn't experience it in a negative way. It startled me with its sudden and apparently random arrival and with its novelty, as it wasn't like anything I'd ever felt before.

Some moments later I was struck with the message carried with its onset: this was a material way for my body to manifest the answer to a question I'd posed to the Entity just the day before. I'd asked, "What is the best thing for me to do to help my healing at this point?" The Entity hadn't answered my question, instead telling me to sit in the current.

Now on my final day at the Casa my question was being answered not in words but expressed in a way I couldn't help but notice and readily understand. My heart needed to open even more and I needed to focus my continuing attentions on giving and receiving love.

Implicit in this message was the need to forgive and offer ongoing compassion to myself as well as all others. It also meant I should continue examining my feelings and long-held beliefs about everything…a task I've tried very hard to bring into my conscious awareness while here. Clearly, I have a lot of inner work still needing to be done.

6

A New (Out of This) Worldview

ONCE UPON A time I hired a contractor to repair a stubborn roof leak. After endless weeks of unsuccessful attempts by the expert to trace and resolve the problem, my frustration increasing at his casual indifference and inability to follow through and pinpoint the source, I again called him out to the house, and after we climbed up onto the roof I turned to him, giving him an opportunity to open the dialogue. Averting my eyes and gazing off into the distance, he repeated his by then infamous introduction, the same phrase I'd heard him intone prior to all his other failed attempts. He said, "You know, I have a theory...." For a final time I reminded him that none of his previous "theories" had sealed the porous membrane, that I wanted results, not his rain-soaked hypotheticals.

Like the theoretical musings of the philosophizing roofer about possible causes there have been many theories about the pathogenesis of my illness. A.L.S. is often referred to as an orphan disease.

This term reflects the fact that due to the relatively small number of people with the malady, many drug companies are reluctant to devote research dollars for an effective treatment when a host of other afflictions offer a much greater potential return on investment. For each theory purporting to have defined the disease's "likely" point of origin, a new breed of pill or even more invasive procedures are developed and touted.

One of my neurologists was all but beside himself shortly following receipt of my original diagnosis when I politely turned down his impassioned plea that I immediately start taking a medication meant to prolong my life. I asked him how long the meds might extend my life and how much the treatment cost...reasonable questions to pose, in my opinion. He answered, "This might *possibly* prolong your life for up to four months." He then said, "It'll cost you about $1,000 per month." I laughed out loud and said, "You've got to be kidding," incredulous at this expensive and absurdly brief palliative. But he wasn't kidding. He was as serious as I was shocked. He was simply doing what he'd been taught to do in medical school: relieve pain and, if not save lives, then at least extend them. As far as my ailment was concerned, he had zero remedies in his pharmacopoeia to assuage either this disorder-without-treatment or the point-of-view of the if not belligerent then at least ungrateful patient before him. That I was questioning his learned counsel raised his professional hackles. I left his office shaking my head in disbelief. What good was four months when what I wanted was forty more years?

• • •

FROM THE TIME I first received my "die"agnosis, my way of being in the world was centered on defiance of the conventional wisdom, logic and historical perspective that collective consciousness brought to bear on the *hopelessness* of my condition. I'd had lots of experience going against the grain of reason and truth, having spent a lifetime in reactive rage against anything contrary to my expectations. Only this time something was different. The *truth* I was being told to accept felt all wrong. Moving forward meant refuting accepted wisdom, thumbing my nose at how society chose to define and pigeonhole terminal illness and those who suffer from it. The signals and messages I continually received all pointed to the futility of my lot, the lunacy of my unconventional treatments half a world away, the utter waste of time and energy misspent in the service of misguided hope and a tragically ill-informed if not woefully blind faith.

The illusion...taken as fact...was that my delusional behavior was typical, a textbook example of homo terminalis. Met with blank stares by those to whom I've told my fantastic tale of Spirit intervention, I both understand their inability to fathom my words and experiences as well as my own desperate need to continue telling my story, my truth of truths. In large part this is why I've never joined support groups. After my disastrous initial introduction to such gatherings I had no further desire to identify more than was absolutely necessary with either the disease or, by extension, those most inclined to compare symptoms while commiserating in a group. While I appreciated their urgent desire to find any new treatment, I'd unwittingly set myself up as an outsider through my all-or-nothing approach to life and by my refusal to allow my situation to be decided by generally accepted opinion.

That may sound snobbish, mean-spirited or grounded in denial, yet I came to realize that the greater the dependence I placed on accepted thinking where my condition was concerned, the less I made myself available to outcomes outside the conventional thought process. While I maintained a profound empathy for my fellow sufferers and supported their right to decide how to confront our mutual nemesis on their own terms, I made the decision to go it alone. By default, I marched to a beat that resonated deep inside. From my vantage point, to do otherwise would risk buying into the entrenched beliefs about the malady's unavoidable path and by association all I held in contempt for how the vast majority viewed and reacted to the label *incurable.*

I didn't deny my diagnosis, however vehemently I defied what was said about it and the potential for locating a non-mainstream cure. I became convinced timelines for survival while statistically compelling tended to mandate finality, the more one accepted the dictates of established societal and medical thinking. I made the decision not to continually remind myself how others chose to view and interpret that which challenged me.

By making this decision I companioned myself to an existence removed from established mainstream circles of support. I brought this isolation on myself, inadvertently operating from my historical obsessive-compulsive mindset. Even though a part of me thrived on a certain degree of aloneness in my pre-disease life, I found this new, insulated landscape almost entirely devoid of meaningful companionship. The nature of my ailment also contributed to this remoteness through my loss of speech. Living with these constraints has often been a very lonely state of being, more purdah-like than anything I'd previously known. In deciding to do this *thing* on my own terms I wasn't at all cognizant of the hardship I was opening myself up to.

I was intent on embracing a new and different thinking concerning the dark flower unfurling deep within. I'd experienced profound inner turmoil at not being able to explain what I'd *witnessed and experienced* to others in ways they could grasp. While I understood their inability to comprehend such an extraordinary context from which to view "reality," it was a frustratingly lonely time that found me on the one hand relishing my newfound connection to the mystical and miraculous and on the other hand unable to give voice... literally and figuratively...to that which held the most meaning and promise for me.

It forced me deep inside myself at a time when I sought nothing so much as the understanding company of others. It forced me to become stronger than I wanted to be at a time when a soft place to fall would've felt a whole lot better. Yet I'd made my bed and now I had to sleep in it. Later I would come to understand that my time away from others provided me what I'd needed most...space to reacquaint myself with who I really was along with the much needed opportunity to discover how to further heal myself.

Unbeknownst to me at that time, my going it alone also represented the ideal circumstance through which to acquire the deep gut-wrenching, soul-searching return to consciousness necessary to my becoming whole again. As the interruptions of the world of illusion slowly gave way in the face of my steady awakening, as I began separating surface manifestation from grace-filled mystery, I no longer had excuses for not engaging myself in the requisite work of peering inside to see truths that had always resided within. Once I was able to accomplish this with some consistency I was prepared to bring my most profound wounds into the light of day and undertake the remedial obligation I was born to fulfill by healing them through a newly opened heart. In the act of losing touch with the world I was able to get in touch with myself for the first time.

However, that heart-healing transformation didn't come about easily. I'd become so inured to the idea of processing my many traumas, I was by now an expert in avoidance. I'd created an almost endless succession of roadblocks to the pursuit of that which, ironically, could redeem me. Any tangent leading away from confronting those dark agonies was worthy of my attention, provided it didn't engender pain...at least greater than that I was already used to in the act of circumventing it.

In hindsight, my shunning these introspective labors induced much greater pain than the original injury ever had. Objective awareness arrived much too late to spare me fresh insult to my original injury. I needed to undergo a transformative awakening formed from the alliance of my long festering wounds with their avoidance in order to grasp what best served rekindled change and its companion growth.

The search for my own saving grace brought me to a wholly unlikely setting and equally improbable hosts, though not to some magical nostrum. It brought me to question the role faith played in my life. It dragged me to a confrontation with the spiritual values permeating every word we utter and every decision we make. I came in search of a miracle, my miracle, and I received it. Only it was an entirely different one than what I'd been looking for.

It began that first day I read the article about Joao de Deus... John of God...and about his special trance mediumship that allowed elevated Spirit Entities to enter and use his physical form to carry out their healing mission on this plane of existence. By the simple act of reading that article, I came into direct contact with those Entities engaging with Spirit's beneficent presence and unknowingly passed through the most spiritually significant portal of my entire life.

The first faint stirrings of faith I experienced while reading about the Casa de Dom Inacio allowed those Entities of light into my life. That inchoate faith, while far from being vital and strong, was enough to energetically summon the Entities to my soul's distress signal. Recalling my Dad's words from beyond this world... "There are no accidents in life...," I saw this watershed event as an act of destiny: a singular rite of passage beckoning me with restorative potential.

• • •

THE UNIVERSE MOVES to a divine syncopation, embodying the *actual* order of every single aspect of creation in utter harmony. The ruse of our collective consciousness, all we blindly accept as real, obscures this *actuality* of truth with the gaudy ornamentation of our fabricated subjective reality, separating us from much deeper levels of understanding by a membrane of unconscious beliefs. These we pathologically fashion into our own personal fairytales of separation, our fables of detachment.

In an environment governed by this same illusion of disconnection and the prejudice it foments, we observe the ceaseless parade of life through rose-tinted glasses, seeing precisely what we've trained our minds to see, only that which supports our beliefs. We create our own personal *sight* either in panoramic or myopic justification to the specific cues carried in our hearts. If our story is one of separation, as mine was, our every thought, word and deed marshals itself to the fulfillment of that unconsciously held intention. The effect is nothing less than allowing ourselves to be misled from the missions our lives were intended to fulfill.

The fabric of my reality was ripped down the middle, exposing me to an infinite backdrop of alternate but viable realities that forced me to re-examine my entire worldview. When I chose to enter this new way of engaging life, synchronicities, intuition, knowings, as well as access to other realms, revealed themselves to me with startling frequency and fullness.

For many years I lived a story of separation and alienation suspended between the given, accepted world and my contrived interpretation of it, as if I'd been in a coma, propelled on the painful tides of the past, stuck in old agonies that comforted me with my victim righteousness, an endless loop tape I could revisit at will to remind myself just how injured I really was. Stockpiling emotional injuries as if they were badges of honor, I basked in an unwavering stubbornness, refusing to relinquish my many fears and unfulfilled expectations, apprehensive of all that lay ahead.

Having to face up to my impending death, I discovered what living meant to me, what being alive allowed me to express and define. I discovered that to be alive…alive in a way whose fullness I'd never fully accessed…was symbolic of the freedom to express myself through needs, desires, rants: the entire cornucopia of emotions… all the feelings I'd never given myself permission to voice, which now constituted the glaringly unrealized aspects of my persona that I wasn't willing to leave this world without expressing.

Garbed in dispiriting cloaks of self-deprivation, fear and a woefully unclear personal philosophy, I allowed myself to be consistently waylaid by an uncertain and diffused sense of self, of where I fit into the world. In the most profound sense my unconscious behaviors allowed life to live me, not the other way around. Death's seeming imminence crystallized my role in the continuum of life. The reality of my looming end caught my attention in a way like nothing else ever had. It was the ultimate reality-check, its utter finality poised to conclude all I'd taken for granted. In this way, the experience of mortality gilds everything you encounter with its urgent, knowing patination. I'd discovered a sobering truth: consciousness of the ways you haven't fully lived increases proportionate to the imminence of your approaching demise.

Once I'd lost everything that defined my pre-diagnosis existence there were no remaining markers to guide me. Traditional, consensus reality options were available but these were marked by the same end-of-the-road finality my diagnosis itself delivered. When Spirit appeared to me through its varied manifestations, it was as if someone threw open a window above and shouted, "Hey, here we are! We can help you. Don't forget us!"

I was initiated into a cult of knowing far more ancient than anything I could grasp. An urgent manifesto called out to me from beyond any known terrain, imploring first that I listen to its message then dedicate myself to the process of awakening I was so graciously being offered. Spirit knew as far as all things spiritual were concerned, my attitude was at best insouciant and at worst disdainful, such was the abhorrence I'd acquired in my parochial upbringing for all the beliefs forced on me with unrelenting fervor.

By swinging open a portal right in front of me at the precise moment when they knew I'd be most receptive, my Spirit intercessors introduced me to a level of awareness and perspective buoyed by their formidable insight which defied anything I'd ever known. Spirit's manifestation by way of channeled communication, direct contact, my *knowings*, shamanic journeywork and access to other levels of awareness in non-ordinary reality all conspired to help me out of the cycle of floundering in past torments, to appreciate and reside in the holy moment and to visualize a future free from constraining self-doubt.

I now thought of my steadily building awakening as a talisman I wore night and day, able to access its revelatory light at any time. Blessed by extraordinary insights I watched myself gradually metamorphose into a new species of empowered being. One example was first discovered in what I came to call my *connectivity*. I reflected in wonder at my ability to successfully diagnose physical problems others were suffering, by accessing *the information field*...the term used to describe the repository of seemingly endless information, the breadth of which I couldn't fully comprehend, yet a force in which I had complete faith.

I didn't consider myself a medical intuitive, for it wasn't really *I* who possessed the capacity to formulate a picture of where in another's physique the imbalance had its origins. Instead it was my ability to *connect* while in a trance state to the universal bank of energetic imprints holding every single thought, word and deed occurring in life on a permanent holographic tapestry that allowed me access to information unavailable in ordinary waking reality.

When I journeyed shamanically or utilized other tools to enter a state of altered consciousness, it was always while holding a clearly stated intention to be *shown* very specific knowledge, guidance and answers. The non-ordinary states of reality I'd learned to enter required focus, directed intention and posing the right kind of questions in order to successfully connect with my Spirit guides and access the *information field*. A vital part of its usefulness was coming to the aid of others, by permitting me to act as a conduit for diagnostic revelations. Just as my path into illness removed me from the comfort of predictability, it also granted me a grace-paved opening into realms of otherness, offering direction and answers wholly unavailable within the limits of the consensus reality I'd adopted as my former truth.

My *connectivity* to other venues of consciousness inside extraordinary reality had nothing to do with occult knowledge, nor did it necessitate special wisdom. By stepping outside accepted reality, I'd been shown how to access other levels of consciousness readily available to each of us. All too often these non-ordinary states are obscured by our tacit acceptance of "approved" existence. Disease yanked me unceremoniously out of my comfort zone, sending me into a free-fall that could only be checked by opening to new ways of viewing existence.

As with all the other introductions to this new spiritual landscape, my time spent with a Russian psychic pushed my awareness of other realms to new heights. A friend mentioned that a professor she knew suggested I seek out the extraordinary abilities of a healer he'd been observing in a clinical study. At the time I was still neck deep in my seeking-after-answers mode so, after hearing more about his particular gift, I invited Yuri* (a pseudonym used to protect privacy) to come to this country and stay in my home while he treated me energetically.

In the process he would also teach me techniques for accessing other levels of consciousness and for healing myself. I weighed what my gut was telling me against the time and energy I was about to commit to the endeavor. I strongly felt that I was being led in this specific direction as opposed to others that hadn't resonated with nearly the same intensity.

Journal entry:

I'd been asked by Yuri, the Russian healer, to "see" and diagnose a friend's daughter's injury. I knew I was being tested to see if I could access the information field. I'd practiced under his tutelage many times prior to this request and had been startled at my success.

I prepared to enter a trance state by centering my attention on my third eye and the space between that center-of-my-forehead point and my pineal gland mid-brain. I "moved" this part of my brain from front to back with each inhalation and exhalation. As I did I went deeper and deeper into a state of profound relaxation.

During the early stages of this relaxation process, as my focused intention steadily intensifies, I gradually sink down into a space where mind loosens its grip and my entire being becomes aware.

As always seems to happen when this process is fruitful I begin to "see" the affected area of the patient come into my trance state field of vision with increasing clarity. It isn't "vision" in the sense of seeing a picture with my eyes or in my mind. Instead it's as if I'm watching a movie which every part of my altered consciousness understands, out of which a specific image comes to life. Often I perceive things not as separate and distinct images but as a whole body "knowing," a form of understanding involving all my senses.

On this occasion the image forming was of the two middle fingers on the girl's left hand. The girl wasn't present during this time but a number of miles away. It seemed curious I was seeing two fingers and not the single affected digit I'd been told to "look" for.

What I "saw" was an injury to the tendon under the middle joint of the finger next to the girl's pinkie finger. The vision of the affected area was very clear. I "knew" the tendon was injured not by its appearance but just spontaneously, convincingly...by some inner "knowing."

The truth of what I was being shown left no room for doubt anywhere in my being. I've never studied human anatomy so I don't have names to attach to what I'm "seeing," only the absolute certainty received along with the image that this is the afflicted area.

Once I received the diagnosis I began a slow, measured return to waking consciousness. When I'd fully wakened from my trance I explained what I'd been shown to the girl's mother. At that point she informed me the problem seemed to be located between the two fingers I'd seen, that they'd taped the two fingers together which explained what I'd observed while in trance.

I never questioned the information I received. I felt its purity and understood its purpose and that was all I really needed to know. As for wondering at its source, I never felt compelled to identify "it" as I was familiar with the Akashic records and felt confident of its existence...whether it was called by that name, known as the information field or referred to by another description. It seemed enough that I was being granted access.

Having effortlessly accessed other levels of reality, my traditional relationship to linear time...past, present, future...began to evaporate, replaced by the sense that all of time was occurring now. I gained the ability not only to understand the past but to change my past just as I was changing my present. My reading in quantum physics supported this dissolution of calendrical measurement. All I was being exposed to in this new course of study provided compelling evidence of the sacred interconnectedness of the material and the immaterial in a free-flowing existential state of oneness.

• • •

WE ARE ALL in the act of becoming something different, participants in the throes of regeneration, our newly forming otherness never separate from our purest form of higher self. While many of us might be unaware of this process, it is ongoing and not merely philosophical premise or the mumbo-jumbo of armchair metaphysicists. It's a gestalt, a continuum of fluid, unrelenting evolution, binding us to growth and change in service to a higher, more sacred ideal.

Whether we know it or not, accept or deny its manifestation, the only constant in life is the unceasingly immutable nature of our soul's quest...its absolute need to grow, commute insolvencies and heal spiritually. For the majority of us the idea of such metamorphosis goes against the great aversion to change we were socialized into believing was a safe and prudent rule of conduct. The conundrum lies in the fact that we cause pain to enter our lives precisely because we go to such great lengths to avoid what we misconstrue to be synonymous with that pain: change...in its fear-laden spectre, in its unfathomable shadows, in its cleansing transmogrification.

From the very beginning my way of being centered on a locus of fear and anxiety, some conscious, yet most of which I remained stubbornly blind to, despite the formidable and almost unrelenting signs of its proximity. My deeply entrenched fears prevented me from gaining first hand knowledge of my deepest feelings. I possessed no viable way to sustain intimacy while the core of my heart was so thoroughly barricaded against any and every imaginable threat. Beyond the dull ache of remembering my formative years, I was captive to a resistance to change, as stubborn as it was consummate. That situation represented a true state of terminal illness in its purest, most deadly form.

Journal entry:

Looking back I see how I gave away my personal power by not voicing my deepest truth. Any power I had was superficial, fleeting, insubstantial...lodged as it was in the outer skin of experience, created through my erroneous perception of what constituted living life.

In place of merely "being false" I'd created a "false being" whose very architecture disallowed investigation of that inner realm where truth commingles with the spiritual imperative of soul.

Complicating this scene was an inner child still trapped by the circumstance of his shuttered life: timid, unsure of himself, emotionally fragile, unable to escape the continual re-wounding that was a condition of his imprisonment.

In spite of my persistently misguided attempts to remain disconnected from my authentic self and, by so doing, to die a little bit more with each new day, I found a way out of the labyrinth. The simple yet profound fact is that, as I write this, I'm nearing the culmination of my seventeenth year living with what I've come to regard not as terminal illness but as a chronic condition. A condition that will in time...soothed by ample doses of patience and faith while undergoing Spirit-initiated mitigation...be alleviated. Even as I peck out these words ever so slowly, I'm awestruck by how far I've come, how long I've survived. How could all six neurologists I consulted have been so wrong? Were they erroneous in their dire predictions concerning my post-diagnosis "short"gevity or did their training simply not include a course in the miraculous?

Journal entry:

How can I ever look at this gift of life in the same way again? I'm no longer the man I was when this odyssey began. I'm forever altered by a new awareness of what life really is and can no longer be the self-limiting person I was for so long. I can never again stifle my emotions and accept the unacceptable. I must embrace healthy catharsis and the truest intent at self-expression. It all boils down to a new order of thinking and of feeling...of listening to what my intuition is telling me in spite of what external conventional wisdoms may direct me to believe. Following the heart and the gut must be my continuing work.

There are many reasons why I've survived as long as I have. Some I understand while other aspects of my passage through this *process* I simply cannot fathom. Yet I do comprehend many of the causes supporting my unprecedented continuing tenure in the flesh. I'm cognizant of these having become a de facto spiritual anthropologist in the process of trodding this insight-laden path recording and cataloging my adventures as they've unfolded and taken on a life of their own. Along the way, by learning how to examine an existence so terribly contrary to truth, I acquired the discipline to transmute ruinous attitudes into those of a healthy psyche.

Though we frequently grouse about life's unfairness and inadequacies, at our deepest core each of us is physiologically hardwired for surviving both the petty and the profound antagonists threatening us. We carry that message in our genetic makeup as surely as we carry the gene for blue eyes or male pattern baldness. After enough time had passed in my post-diagnosis survival for me to guardedly wonder at my remarkable continuance, I reflected on the elements sparking my ability to endure. Certainly possessing a strong will and an equally strong connection to the healing spirit Entities of the Casa were chief among factors contributing to my still being alive.

Yet what powered my uninterrupted presence in the flesh was something vastly more potent. It was a commodity emblematic of my entire lifelong struggle to regain what I'd always lacked. I'm speaking of love. Paradoxically, though I was grossly deficient in self-love at the time I maintained an overwhelming love for my son. It was an incredibly vigorous force with a life of its own, unqualified and unconditional, a presence deep within my heart...whole, natural, extraordinary, unlike any emotion I'd ever experienced. I cherished my son and frequently stood in awe at the power and purity of my feelings for him. I considered him a very special gift, a gift in fact that was the motivation for my newly-found desire for prayer, pushing up as it did through the hardened surface of my near-epic religious disaffection. My concern for his well-being caused me to take up prayer as a means of petitioning for his care during a time of tremendous emotional upheaval.

Through the trials of divorce and in the subsequent suspension of anything vaguely resembling a normal father-son relationship, my heart ached for my child and the vital connection we'd enjoyed.

Forces conspired to keep us apart, post-divorce, that were capricious, misguided and based in anger, rage and resentment. Little could be done at the time to turn that situation around. Just as I seemed incapable of rescuing him from deprivation my love for him grew stronger and stronger. Each day I'd send him all the love I knew for him from the same heart that ached at our forced disconnection. *For that was the sole remaining power I possessed.*

And in the most real sense imaginable, it was this very love that propelled me through the darkest, lowest points in my odyssey. While I could see the pain etched on his face from the tumult occupying his mind and heart, I knew that transmitting love to him energetically each day *meant* something positive to his spiritual welfare and served to fortify his heart and soul. Without realizing it, his shining presence in my life played a dramatic role in saving my life. I know equally my prayers of love helped him as he struggled to separate bias from truth, as we each embarked on our not dissimilar narratives of diminishment and separation.

Against the larger backdrop of day-to-day life, extramundane events continued appearing with increasing regularity, illuminating my journey in ways no earthly experience ever could. This allowed me insights and stability unavailable in the ordinary life I left behind. My experiences to date dissuade me from concluding that chance or luck have determined my good fortune and longevity. Chance has no viable place in my personal belief system, punctuated as it's been by consistent communication and direction from healing spirit Entities, where faith and intention commingle with the knowledge that one's path is part kismet, part choice.

• • •

THE SPIRIT ENTITIES of the Casa de Dom Inacio continue to work at turning off the switch that flipped on in my genes at the inception of the illness. When I'm at the Casa, their labors on behalf of my ongoing cure are active and very noticeable. When I'm away from these aggressive energetic treatments I'm on a kind of maintenance regimen often supported by the Entity- prescribed herbs. Although I feel their proximity, it's in a more passive manner. I've come to view my time away from the Casa as a spiritual mandate, an opportunity to expand on lessons received while present in that rarified atmosphere. And past their actively working at the stuff of mending my material self, I've come to view these off-premises assignments as homework for the soul...my responsibility in furthering self-restoration.

Altering my old patterns, behaviors and the very way I engage life are *key elements* fostering my return to wholeness. Thus the Entites do their part to support my unfolding miracle and I do mine. If I'd only possessed the will to survive absent Spirit intercession, I have little doubt that I would've died long ago. Cemeteries are full of people just as determined as I've been that they wouldn't allow their illness to make them just another statistic. My mission in this body and in this world aren't finished yet. Otherwise I would've returned to the other side by now. I'm quite literally grateful beyond words to be allowed more time to finally identify and complete my real work, just as I'm excited at the prospect of discovering and fulfilling my highest, most meaningful purpose.

Journal entry:

I spent a very enlightening spiritual healing session several days ago with a woman who's a very gifted medium, one who'd been approved by the Casa Entities. She conducted the session in her home here in this small village of tired and worn adobe brick houses.

She had me lay on a tall table...a chore getting me up onto, even with my assistant's formidable strength. Quiet Eastern sounding music played softly in the background as she told me to close my eyes and relax. I breathed deeply and slowly and soon found myself releasing tension as I drifted into a soft, deep state of peace-filled relaxation.

She began the treatment by invoking the presence of spirit Entities she worked with and Jesus Christ, asking them to guide her in her work. She placed crystals on my sixth chakra, fourth chakra and third chakra. Then she began to very lightly massage different points on my head, neck, shoulders and chest in a fashion quite similar to how cranio-sacral practitioners lightly move their hands over the cranium and neck of a patient.

When she arrived at my arms she pressed down more firmly over their entire length and pressed the joints of my hands and straightened out my now almost constantly curled fingers. She then swept her hands down the length of my arms again as if gathering negative energies and moving them down and off of my body. As she started work on my legs she repeated a similar gesture with a sweeping motion.

During her work as I went deeper and deeper into altered consciousness I began to see an image slowly forming. It was of my mother's face, a face I hadn't seen in ten years since she lay on a bed in the hospital shortly before passing away, ravaged by the cumulative effects of decades spent tormented by diabetes.

Yet in this vision she possessed the face she had in her mid-30's... young, beautiful, brimming with energy and health. I saw only her face suspended before me in mid-air. She spoke just five words to me. She said in a soft, loving voice: "You will be healed, darling." Then her presence was gone. She's not appeared to me since. I have no doubt she "came through" due to the medium's strong connectivity coupled with my own psychic receptivity.

Her brief but love-filled presence was a powerful continuation of Spirit messages, which I've been blessed to receive from many different sources since beginning this odyssey. This provides me with still more evidence of the importance of seeking Spirit through all available channels of light. My mother's message was another reminder to me to continue my journey with faith and patience.

"Everything happens for a reason" became my motto as I continued laboring at what for me was the counter-intuitive work of letting-go. By this point I couldn't overlook the sheer number of times beneficent Spirits had sought me out to deliver a simple five word statement like my mother had or an evocative depiction of his life and after-life as my father had done. Spirit guides scolded my laziness, I experienced lucid visions while sitting in the current at the Casa, I readily accessed the information field while in a trance state, I connected with powerful spirit mentors while journeying shamanically, my clairsentient *knowings* arrived with ever increasing frequency.

My life became a study in observing what Spirit communication, alternate reality or psi phenomena would manifest next. I began thinking of myself as a *numenographer*, a word I coined to better describe the process I was now engaged in, as my journal swelled with daily entries of expanding mystical adventures. The following relates a shamanic journey I took to engage one of my guides in answering an important question.

Journal entry:

I invoked my private and sacred place...the Neah Bay tidal pool from which I've begun my journeys previously...a warm, quiet spot baked by the sun, filled with wondrous, brightly colored creatures. I lay on my back in this pool, relaxed deeply over a period of some minutes and was carried up into the clouds and the upper world by an immense waterspout.

I found my Spirit guide, Stephen, and immediately asked him the question I'd decided to focus on: "What is the next step to take in healing myself?" He answered emphatically, kindly and without hesitation:"loving yourself."

What followed was his further explanation of this point, yet everything he stated after his initial succinct two-word response was just reinforcement of that original reply. I didn't hear his response with my ears; I felt his words permeate my entire being energetically.

I asked him if he would show me his face this time. He answered by turning to face me directly. I was astonished to see he had the face of Christ. He offered that Christ's face is the true face of every person. Seeing his face and hearing his words touched me profoundly.

We began to walk...largely in silence...with him reminding me from time to time as I endeavored to ask him other questions: "Just concentrate on loving yourself...on fully and completely accepting yourself for who you are right now...especially with your current physical problems."

On my journeys the presence of information materializes in a sort of implicit understanding that seems voice-like in its conviction. That may be another way of saying "telepathic."

I then heard the drumbeat and easily returned to the tidal pool.

These were extraordinary times of profound experiential insight and growth. I underwent dramatic shifts in awareness as my worldview lurched and wobbled on its axis from one dramatically prodded repositioning to the next. Often a period of concentrated, spiritually seismic activity would be followed by a void, absent any heightened receptivity whatsoever. I came to see these seemingly fallow interim stages as times to assimilate all I'd just received.

The fact that nothing faintly resembling these spectral nudges had ever happened to me before suggested that my *sensing* apparatus...my spiritual antennae...were in a state of such profound neglect the signal was simply not getting through. Equally true was that those I couldn't see operated from a plan I really couldn't begin to comprehend. Regardless of the reasons contributing to my previous inability to connect with these forces, the wondrous thing was that I was now intimately joined to unparalleled transcendent energies, dramatically transforming my life. I felt unconditional love emanating from these vehicles of discernment as I felt them usher me into the midst of sacred connectedness.

Journal entry:

This whole concept of faith is an intriguing one for me. What's always informed me on an intuitive level from the beginning of these challenging past few years has been this very strong sense I would eventually find a way back to health.

This sensation...admittedly partly the earnest hope of someone not yet ready to leave this planet and partly the inner knowing that my destiny didn't necessarily need to follow a fate predicted and predictable...combined to form a palpable truth, yet one not readily definable in logical terms.

Having heard the Entity, himself, tell me on more than one occasion he would heal me, confirmation of those initial deep-seated stirrings, of sensing the presence of a formula for my salvation, is becoming reality.

Problems arise when I allow my head to get in front of my heart, when my mind dictates control measures as a way to continue validating all those years of left brain training that, until recently, governed every facet of my life. The wonderful lesson is obvious: there's a rhythm and a timing appropriate to all things...my healing included.

If I choose to try and force this natural cadence off its normal path I mess with the equation that allows for the most probabilities in the universe to come to my aid....to manifest their natural order of healing. If, rather, I understand what needs to occur without meddling I aid and abet my rejuvenation tremendously. All of these threads lead back to faith.

By way of my own experiences I arrived at the realization that untested faith is unformed and incomplete, a weak imposter. It can be discussed, philosophized about, even made to seem convincingly resolute. In my process of awakening I discovered that what I'd thought of as my own strong faith was nothing more than a permeable, transitory veneer, prone to crack under real challenge, a badge that while worn credibly, provided nothing in the way of lasting resolve when the going got tough.

All the discord I'd encountered served to test my spiritual resolve while conferring on it those compulsory tribulations necessary to shape it into a stalwart, not easily forsaken presence. Out of this union of contrariness...faith vs doubt...sprang a faith *mentored* by doubt. Uncertainty furnished faith with just the grist necessary for the spirit mill's most vital operation as is clear in the following.

Journal entry:

When we went before the Entity today he took one look at the kind interpreter who'd posed my query to him ["Do I have A.L.S. or is it something else?"] and said matter-of-factly: "Why does he need to know this when I am curing him?"

I had to return to my seat and ask myself (once again!?) which "f" word was I going to choose from here on out: fear or faith?

7

The Well of Emptiness

MY GREATEST, MOST persistent challenge remains the constant frustration insinuating itself into every nook and cranny of my day. It's a cumulative consequence of myriad rituals for which the spirit is willing but the flesh now too weak to oblige. The perception stubbornly dominating my thoughts is that if I used to be able to complete a movement autonomically for the first forty-five years of my life I should still be able to muster what's necessary to do so now. Even after all these years expended in bondage to the constraints of disease I'm so programmed mentally to the thought of automatic movement, to what *should* be present, I'm still genuinely surprised it's now inconsistent, if not entirely absent. Being continually reminded of my inability to complete so many basic, taken-for-granted tasks lies at the center of frustration's ever near proximity…a taunting presence I absolutely despise.

Having to be dressed and undressed, having meals prepared in tall-sided plastic bowls more easily grasped by weak, misshapen and unwilling fingers, having to be raised and lowered from the toilet…these and a hundred other similar daily duties act as unceasing reminders of what separates me from what I once thought of as normalcy. They challenge me physically and psychologically.

As onerous as these things are, my missing voice remains the primary catalyst for frustration. It separates me from others isolating me from the dialogue we all thrive on. At an intrinsic level, life revolves around speaking one's mind. Participating in the varied intimacies of the socialization process requires a vocal identity. Words propelled my thoughts and ideas on an emotional trajectory aimed at seeking communal resonance with others. Speaking was involuntary, assured, seemingly indelible in its capacity to express and in its ability to persist. Verbal expression confirmed the essential imprint I made, serving as a reminder of my role in what continues. Absent fluid communication, an integral tool was lost alienating me from others.

The dispossession I feel, being bereft of voice, is brought into focus most profoundly when I'm attempting to communicate through the use of "after-the-fact" vehicles of transmission: things like my portable alphabet board, fingerspelling, pecking out words on my TV screen and even resorting to email as a followup means of expressing what can't be conveyed face-to-face. None of these tools allow for spontaneity in dialogue and certainly not the speed at which a typical conversation is conducted.

For people unschooled in my plodding attempts at disjointed monologue, the Herculean effort required to patiently stand by while I point at i-n-d-i-v-i-d-u-a-l letters on my alphabet board to form basic words or hunt and peck on my keyboard to form even rudimentary messages only serves to heighten their already taxed staying power. They can't wait to resume normal conversation unfettered by such mind-numbing roadblocks to the automatic flow of words.

Sensing their need to return to a world unchallenged by silence, by such tortoise-like means of expression, I've learned to be empathetic. Each time a pause in the normal flow of language occurs as I grope for the most readily available means of communication, I re-experience the void my missing speech creates. I prepare for these situations by considering them a meditation in remaining calmly centered: not so much enduring their little agonies as rising above being dumbstruck, to connect with the peace at my core. I know from practice that taking this approach will soothe the savage beast of anger poised to gnaw at my tenuous patience.

One by-product of being mute is that I've begrudgingly become more accepting of my isolation from society. Even when surrounded by others, in the give and take act of conversing at some point, it's simply a lot easier, less tiring and so much less frustrating (ah, that word again....) to acquiesce to the estrangement foisted on me by the circumstance of my communication embargo.

I often reflect on whether I'm giving up or just momentarily giving in where my speechlessness and other limitations are concerned. Either way I feel the isolation in the core of my being as a heavy, unwelcome weight. As the years have passed, my existence feels increasingly remote, sometimes bordering on obscurity and, in spite of the Entity's repeated admonitions that I'm healing, remains pointed in the direction of continuing deterioration, an entropic consequence wrought by physical challenge, the continuation of symptoms and through increasing emotional isolation. My rite of passage through a decade and a half of adversity has delivered me to a point where I'm often floundering through a relentless undercurrent of alienation and separation...old companions challenging me within a new circumstance...whose presence conveys lessons from long ago.

Even with new coping strategies to counter what's simultaneously unacceptable and reality, I'm unable to get beyond one basic fact. Being deprived of spoken language and the deep sense of belonging it fosters disturbs me. Having few alternative modes of engaging others freely is a deprivation I liken to solitary confinement. The silence of my muted presence often sounds deafening, as if it possesses an audible quality I alone can hear. It encloses me in a cocoon that might as well be floating aimlessly through space for all the disconnection from everyday conversation and life. As robust as my spirit is, this is the kind of dispossession capable of shattering my very center.

I'm conscious of a parallel reality at work here, too. Because I can't rely on the normal, automatic mechanism of speech, I've been forced in all my countless hours of solitude to finally gaze inside myself, to discover and confront the truth. I continually remind myself it's within such verbal disenfranchisement that the brilliant purpose of self-discovery and self-healing has been so well served.

• • •

ONE BRIGHT WINTER morning I experienced one of those epiphanies I'd grown accustomed to having seep into my consciousness. Like so many other *knowings* it came to me upon first waking when I was just alert enough to understand I was straddling two levels of awareness, still in a hypnopompic state yet overlapping different spheres of consciousness. This point of convergence had consistently provided access to insights unavailable on the normal, waking plane of existence.

In this space I clearly saw that hiding just behind frustration's unending nuisance lay the resolve and serenity needed to turn around how I'd been interacting with its debilitating presence. I could turn the tables on what I'd come to view as my foe. Instead of continually reacting to its repeated incursions into my very sanity I could harness its energy and absorb what it had been trying to teach me all these years.

This novel awareness built on the "calm center" meditation I'd begun using in the midst of my achingly slow attempts at communicating. I adopted a different mindset, grounded in a disciplined letting-go, in order to free myself of the expectations-fueled premise I'd somehow be magically released from its torment one day. I knew from experience any attempts to suppress it would have the same effect as indulging it. It was time to learn from it. That could only happen by being proactive.

This was no lightning flash of satori but the continuation of my slow, steady awakening. The more I drew these experiences in non-ordinary realms to me, the stronger I grew, the more real and authentic I felt myself become. Put another way, I was at last discovering what my authentic self really looked like. I knew there were truths scattered all around...most notably inside me...if I could only learn to access them. I sensed their beckoning presence and felt a compelling tug urging me to redouble my efforts to continue moving deeper into the process of growth. This involved willingly seeing things in a new light in place of merely judging them by surface appearance. It also required opening my heart and abandoning a long-held resistance to change. Forsaking the falsehoods of polarity, duality and separation went against everything I'd ever learned about life. Ultimately it became a battle pitting inertia against my will to transform myself. And so I gradually learned to make peace with a war I could never win, only continue waging, but now on terms of my own choosing. That was enough.

Now for much the same reason I'd consciously chosen not to dwell on my symptoms or join support groups (I had no interest in *supporting* accepted wisdom on the subject of my illness but rather finding ways to harness what it was there to teach me) I made the choice to turn around these feelings of frustration, anger, aloneness and even rage. In place of endlessly feeding them, I began to extract from them any balm of succor and insight within the nucleus of their pain. This wasn't so much a cerebrally focused plan of attack as it was a spiritually motivated imperative. I had to do it if I expected to remain sane. It was that simple. And yet, I was only successful in momentarily stemming the tide of frustration's implacable march. The remaining battles with my tutoring nemesis centered on trying to curtail its momentum. If I could gain even transient reprieve from its numbing encroachment into the warp and weft of my daily existence, I'd consider it a triumph over circumstance.

While the choice not to partake in support groups seemed simple enough, it brought with it complex repercussions. My higher self chose isolation because it represented the best way for my soul to discover what my heart lacked almost from the beginning. That realization, coming long after the fact, offered little mitigation from my suffering. Yet it put into perspective some of the reasons behind the direction in which I was now thankfully headed.

If there was a single redemptive salve that oiled my intent it was the act of invocation, prayer and speaking with Spirit daily. Over a period of several years as I watched to see what would happen from my new dialogue with Source I was continually rewarded. I asked, pleaded and implored God, my Spirit guides and my benefactors, the spirit Entities of the Casa de Dom Inacio, to guide me and light my path with the insight and intuition I so desperately sought and needed. I returned to prayer ever so haltingly after my painful early experiences in the 50's and 60's.

For many years I was only able to muster the briefest attempts at talking to God, so strong was my abhorrence at reliving those memories. I re-engaged with sacred petitioning very slowly, hesitant to churn up recollections better left undisturbed. The fact is, I'd always felt completely detached from Whomever it was up there in that place called heaven. When I saw that creating a new beginning through prayer was both possible and indispensable, I was able to move beyond childhood agonies and long held biases and assume true responsibility for my actions moving forward.

In defining the purpose of my orisons I created for the first time an honest, open channel to Source, at once deeply meaningful and refreshingly untainted by the bias of religious ideology. Prayer propelled me closer and closer to my true spiritual purpose, helping me through the innumerable hours, days, weeks and months of abject, utter aloneness. Although it's been said that it's never too late to have a happy childhood, looking at, dealing with and finally overcoming one of the primary sources of so much of my childhood angst and pain was monumentally challenging. Yet without doing so, I would remain unfulfilled, incomplete and less than victorious in my efforts to transcend the unconsciousness I'd acted out almost my entire life.

• • •

I WANTED SO badly to taste words again, to savor their singular textures as they slid glossally and gutturally across my palate. Dysarthria, a by-product of A.L.S., prevented me from speaking clearly and being understood. As the disease slowly progressed, my speech slowly regressed. Only my son seemed able to comprehend what came out of my mouth, somehow making sense out of thick, garbled sounds, mining if not a literal translation, then at least the gist of what I was trying to say. If I was going to continue "talking," it would need to take place through mental mimicry, a kind of piggybacking onto words others vocalized, hitchhiking on the vehicle of voice containing their consonants and vowels. While this constituted a poor alternative for the real thing it kept me in touch with what I still earnestly desired.

I often did this during the prayers recited at the end of the sessions while in the current at the Casa, mouthing each syllable as I tried to remember what speech felt like. Aside from silently sitting there in my wheelchair, it was another way to show God and its spirit Entities I held a fervent intention and a sizeable desire to once again one day join my voice to the masses. Prayer, newly re-discovered, seemed the *only* appropriate vehicle through which to simultaneously offer *gratitude* for all I'd been given, while recalling the rhythms and sounds of language that had been taken away.

During this pivotal time I received constant guidance from the Spirit world, much of it directly, at other times indirectly through intuition and further development of my *knowings*. I began trusting my intuitive powers and watched in awe as the clairsentient, empathic aspect of my being...my mediumship...began to develop. I was more deeply connected to a part of me I'd never dreamed existed as I became aware that I could *feel* the energies of others. I often *knew* by some mysterious process what others were feeling and even the emotional problems they were experiencing.

I refused to attach labels to this awareness, because I'd become wary of the plethora of individuals advertising themselves as "healers," a term too often and too easily subjectified into meaning more than it actually did. I am not a healer, unless you consider my ongoing endeavors at self-healing to fall under that general rubric. I'm learning the gift of clairsentience a bit at a time, a novice practitioner sometimes tentative in trusting what it tells me, observing it with childlike eyes filled with wonder and awe. Now, as I look back at my life, I'm able to see many instances where I felt the presence of this benediction yet simply didn't know what it was, nor what I should do with it.

Journal entry:

I sat in the first current room, the medium's room, through which everyone passes on their way to see the Entity. After I'd closed my eyes I rapidly entered a deep trance state similar to ones I enter when doing shamanic journeywork or accessing the Akashic records. Once I began to feel myself drifting towards familiar terrain I let go trusting in wherever it might take me while observing what I was being led to.

At first I left my body and drifted high above the earth, completely wrapped in a violet colored cocoon. As this experience unfolded it didn't gather strength and solidify but became indistinct, slowly drifting out of my awareness.

After this sensation I felt the presence of an angel sitting in my wheelchair with me in the current, literally superimposed onto my own form like a hologram. It had tremendous wings and robes of shimmering white cloth. I instantly "knew" its name in my altered perceptual awareness. It was a being named Marion, a female energy. She let me understand she was always with me, guiding me, lighting the way for me.

This was a glorious revelation coming on the heels of my efforts these past several weeks to invoke Spirit...having asked for guidance not solely from the Entities at the Casa de Dom Inacio but from my Spirit guides, Spirit mentors and guardian angels as well.

This couldn't have been a more direct response to my prayers and, although not surprising given my prior connection to Hector and to my father's Spirit, confirmation of what I'd been told early on: "You've got to feed the Spirits. If you don't they'll just forget about you."

I consider this another positive omen of things to come. My burgeoning connection to the realm of Spirit strengthens each day. I've *discovered formidable guidance is readily accessible. All that separates me from communicating with those on the other side is effort, focus and determination.*

I've a strong sense...a *knowing*...that part of my purpose in wearing a suit of flesh this time around is to help others heal. I don't yet know precisely how I'm meant to do this but don't doubt for a moment the direction will be revealed to me at the right time. I'm quick to remind myself I'm not a healer. While others possess that gift I'm simply a willing vessel Spirit can use to help others. Time will tell whether or not I'm destined to be a *conduit* for healing. Having trekked through my own valley of shadows for so long and come out on the other side renewed, awakened and conscious has bestowed a certain perspective not readily obtainable by other means. My wish is that my odyssey will help others heal by giving credence to the notion that anything is possible. Or as a Chinese proverb states: "People who say it cannot be done should not interrupt those doing it."

I started this book initially to chart where I'd gone wrong in life. It was a way of coming to grips with what needed to be done to heal all the discord I'd created. Writing acted as a catharsis to purge my sizeable pain while mending dissonant behaviors. During its evolution I discovered it could also serve as a template to help guide others who don't know where to turn in a time of crisis.

Journal entry:

The wind outside the door to my room at the pousada here in Abadiania is tormenting everything in its turbulent path. The branches of the tall abacate (avocado) tree whiplash with gusts that rise and fall at no precise intervals sending the grouped clusters of swelling fruit seesawing to and fro in a frenetic dance.

Today, Saturday, the first day following the end of the weekly sessions at the Casa, is a day when I do little...confined to quarters by lack of mobility and the hours-long absence of my helpers in the interim between lunch and dinner. It's become a time of naps... because they're mandated by the Entity as a crucial part of my return to health....and because my body hasn't been bashful about sending me the message that it needs rest, rest and more rest.

— 125 —

In these sleep-laden moments I've discovered I'm often writing a book as if another part of my consciousness is dictating the words, the chapter headings, the main ideas, etc. This is a recurring dream of mine, a fascinating process to participate in as it arrives in my consciousness automatically, unbidden.

I'm left with several realizations: The journey I've been on since late 1995, when I first begin to notice a slight catch in my voice, is compelling enough to cause my subconscious mind to sort and arrange the various parts of this unfolding story in such a way that they come into my resting mind's eye often with startling clarity.

There's a singular voice emerging from these adventures that's more focused than any I've witnessed before. This voice seems inspired by my connectivity to the realm of Spirit in that it fulfills a message to help others, is informed by unconditional love and by the genuine desire to provide assistance.

The process of writing brings me to a direct confrontation with those parts of my heart and psyche which require healing. Writing puts me in touch with myself in ways that nothing else does.

The only other time I consciously recall being possessed of such clarity while writing was when a poem of mine, published when I was a college student, "came" to me in the same way. That poem flew into my head and was utterly complete in the moment between arriving in consciousness and being written down. I marveled as much at the process as I did at the finished product.

Having read "The Spirit's Book" and "The Medium's Book" by Allan Kardec I've become aware of the reasons motivating how we receive intuition. These perceptions have expanded my understanding from whence creativity really springs.

It's in this light that I know our connectedness to the Spirit realm is strong and real, that much of what we write off as inspiration are, in fact, subtle messages sent from another place. In similar fashion a thought we already have can be heightened and expanded by a Spirit who finds it appropriate to come to our assistance at *that point in time to benefit our acquisition of some new piece of knowledge.*

• • •

MY DAY OFTEN begins with receipt of new ideas and clarification of what I've previously pondered and written. As I lie in bed in that half awake, half asleep hypnopompic state I've come to recognize and cherish as a form of channeling, I'm often furnished deep levels of discernment and guidance. This point of entry into the morning has become second nature to me. In it I obtain *information* not readily summonable in the flow of normal waking consciousness. And although it doesn't occur with clockwork regularity it's become an important beginning to days too often devoted to the continuing struggle with my adversary who, in life's exquisitely paradoxical way, doubles as my mentor.

Its easy to allow myself to get waylaid in the service of writing out instructions for those caring for me. I've become an unintentional expert in how others process the written word, frequently struggling through a hurried, uncareful reading of my seemingly clear, detailed messages or laboring under varying levels of misinterpretation. The bright spot in this lies in the fact that I'm compelled to grow more empathetic toward others and myself, to continually revisit my practice of patience as well as to learn to write with greater clarity and concision if I wish to be understood. I'm constantly surprised by just how much time I devote to this necessary evil. Yet, when viewed from the vantage point of how it's informed who I'm becoming, there's no substitute for its revelations.

As I began living in two completely different worlds, other valuable insights washed over me. My life stateside had become a predictable, carefully orchestrated series of assisted tasks...centered in my compulsive yet necessary list-making...interrupted by solo time when my various caregivers were absent. After many years companioned to physical challenge I had my day largely down to a science.

This structure provided me and my aides the ability to rely on a much needed routine.

It also had the less desirable effect of leaching out any remaining spontaneity, a casualty of the war I was waging to exert some hint of control in my little cosmos. I often felt isolated from nurturing contact with accepted reality, ultimately learning how to brave my silent little perch with pursuits resonating inside me. While these activities tethered me to a sense of purpose and substance, they offered little in the way of the deep spiritual sustenance that remained truant from my heart. As C.C. Jung put it: *"Loneliness does not come from having no people about one, but from being unable to communicate the things which seem important to oneself, or from holding certain views which others find inadmissible."*

In the absence of being surrounded by others who've also experienced the transcendent phenomenon found at the Casa de Dom Inacio or in similar experiences, I often felt out of place in an environment unable to fathom the extent of what was *really* going on, in and out of this world. I struggled with the sheer weight of remarkable new knowledge, not due to its content so much as its difficulty in being conceptualized by others operating outside such a framework of experiential reference. I'd been granted unrestrained access and insight into levels of extraordinary reality, the likes of which provided me information and perspective unavailable within the confines of consensus reality's assumptions.

The spiritual climacteric I was now engrossed in required that I abandon the lingering taint of old, comfortable thinking where the numinous was concerned, in favor of literally living the new truth I'd been shown. I'd been entrusted with discrete knowledge as difficult for most to believe as is my own unprecedented healing. I saw the futility of trying to win over others to my utterly fantastic story, those who hadn't *experienced* what I had and were in no way prepared for a challenge to the belief system they'd adhered to for a lifetime. Any attempts on my part would be no different from what the nuns in grade school tried to do to convert me to their system of belief. Such forcibly fed inducements had only succeeded in causing me to turn a deaf ear to their impassioned pleas.

I'd spend seven months or so in my stateside home, then venture south to Brazil and the spiritual healing center where I'd spent so many hours in service to my continued healing. Brazil was the right-brain counterpoint to my left-brain life lived in a North American city. Brazil was intuitive, creative and deeply spiritual, the vast majority of whose people existed simultaneously in poverty and faith: the latter revealing intrinsic meaning in the presence of the former. For all its wealth and swagger, life stateside seemed possessed of problems it shouldn't have, while to the average Brazilian problems were as prevalent as their penchant for sweets. Living in two such divergent settings gave me a sobering perspective on how cultures define their identities. My twin existence also helped me identify my own values in a new and different light.

• • •

EVEN WITH MY substantial physical challenges I have trouble imagining what it must be like for the person afflicted with more advanced stages of A.L.S. Existing in a body that will neither move nor obey the dictates of a mind otherwise untouched by the ravages of the disease is a trial of almost unimaginable proportions-even to someone like me, as deeply cognizant as I am of the difficulties, trying to live with this debilitating illness.

At the pleading of a mutual friend I met one such person in the city of Anapolis in Brazil in 2005. Once a big strapping man well over six feet tall and 220 pounds he was a shrunken husk of his former self when compared to bedside photographs. He was confined to a hospital bed in a room of his lavish home, overlooking beautiful tropical gardens and a large swimming pool. He was hooked up to a bi-pap machine which breathed for him in the absence of his ability to do so. Like me he'd lost close to fifty pounds off his big-boned frame. He could only open and close his eyes, his sole remaining means of signaling others when he needed something.

He now lived in the grasp of "locked-in syndrome," his mind functioning perfectly inside a body no longer capable of movement. His wife, clearly burdened by his care and the spectre of what seemed inevitable, asked our mutual acquaintance how long I'd had the disease. Her husband had been stricken just two short years prior to this advanced state. She'd watched me closely as my aide had helped me out of our taxi into a standing position then supported my left arm while I'd used a cane clutched in my right hand to slowly walk the 30 yards from the vehicle to his bedroom.

When my friend answered, "*Mais que oito anos agora,*" (more than eight years ago now) I watched the poor woman's face change expression from one of bereavement to utter incredulity. She looked directly into my eyes and bluntly asked in her native Portuguese, "Are you absolutely certain you have A.L.S.?" Through my friend, I assured her that three separate neurologists had confirmed my diagnosis. Even at hearing this she asked me the question twice more, so unbelieving was she that this could be the same illness her husband suffered from.

Later, as I replayed the scene again in my mind, I reflected on the similarities and differences joining and separating the two of us. We were virtually the same age, one on the brink of leaving his body, the other surviving beyond the average while continuing to function at a high level. I nodded to myself knowingly...gratefully. I've never made a secret of ascribing my longevity to having begun treatments early on at the Casa de Dom Inacio under the care and guidance of my discarnate consulting Spirit physician, Dr. Algosto de Almedia. I am as certain of the fact that this is why I'm alive today as I am of eventually being cured of the incurable. For God, working through his intermediaries of light, nothing is impossible.

As in the case of the gentleman sharing my diagnosis, if there is anything bittersweet in meeting and bonding with so many different people at the Casa de Dom Inacio it's that some of them come there as a last resort in end-stage circumstances. They're often beyond a physical cure. In that sacred place of the miraculous, I've watched many good souls struggle in their final weeks of life. In losing them as friends I've gained fresh perspective on what death really is, on the survival of death by the eternal soul and what it means to possess the gift that is this essence called life. I've asked Spirit why I've survived against all odds while others have returned to the other side. I've pondered how I'm meant to give back to others to try and repay the indebtedness I feel toward my Spirit benefactors. I know I'm being guided in discovering my true purpose and the answers to these questions.

Throughout this steadily expanding journey of self-discovery I've become a student of the power of faith and belief in the face of ponderous adversity. My faith has been severely tested, been horribly shaken and, ultimately, after being continuously pommeled, become an almost invincible pillar of resilience. If my faith hadn't repeatedly been put to the test, I'd never have experienced those dark nights of the soul that inform who I am today. In other words, I needed to manifest doubt and fear in order to learn how to truly believe and exactly what it was I believed in. Doubt and fear continue to test me sometimes getting the upper hand. In the presence of my faith, though, it's a temporary victory at best.

I'd learned circumstance can affect one's "faith receptors" providing compelling reasons to dissuade a person from trusting that their causal link with Source is enough to sustain them during crisis. My mind, joined to an intransigent ego, struggled for the right direction in which to turn, even though the answers coming from my manic, unfocused obsession with staying alive were the product of reflexively grasping at *anything* that might save me. Like the ouroboros...the ancient symbol of a serpent swallowing its own tail...I was only consuming my own valuable energy in a frantic dash to preserve myself. In that state of mind I was torn between allowing faith to sustain me versus clamoring after any modality which promised even the slimmest illusion of a cure. If I was going to survive this epic tug-of-war it would require getting very clear in mind and heart about *why* I wished to survive. For without a substantive purpose for remaining in this life, any enduring I might accomplish would ring as hollow as the reality of unconsciousness I now labored to escape.

I'm being cured of an "incurable," terminal disease while actively engaged in determining the positive outcome of that cure. This isn't a snap-your-fingers quick healing but...as the Entity stated...an incremental alleviation of imbalances in my spiritual, mental, emotional and physical bodies, the combined resolution of which will deliver me to homeostasis. In the process, my various energy bodies come into increasingly better alignment as I continue learning my lessons and institute the requisite changes.

I'm a hands-on participant in what for most is simply *impossible:* an unprecedented return to wellness. To the degree I expend the effort and absorb the various teachings my soul is here to experience, my soul followed by my body heals proportionate to my exertion. Without my faith and belief and fervent desire to be well, none of this would be possible. Without Spirit present to guide, instruct and scold me I'd never have discovered the roots of my unwellness, nor the means to heal.

I subscribe with every facet of my being to the biology of hope and faith. There is no doubt in my mind and in my heart...in fact in my very cells...of its efficacy in the healing process. I breathe in that ardent intention with each new day I'm given. I subscribe to the universal laws of attraction, drawing subtle energetic reinforcement to myself throughout the day by evoking an attitude of presumptuous positivity. While English teachers everywhere might cringe at that alliterative logjam, it's a simple mnemonic tool to help me remain conscious of the need to continuously monitor my thoughts and emotions. And, of course, I often fail, choosing anger, frustration and impatience over their polar cousins...a continual reminder that the eternal soul's residence is, after all, a temporal wrapper with its inconsistencies, imperfections and illusions.

As a direct consequence of espousing this philosophy of hope, I stubbornly refused to buy into the prevailing "wisdom" concerning my prognosis. While most everyone could enjoy a field day coming up with reasons motivating that decision...aside from the simple fact I wanted to stay alive...there were a series of events that cascaded sequentially as well as synchronistically, leading me to one right choice after another.

Any survival decision begins with a plan of action, a strategy to succeed no matter the odds. I knew in my gut from the beginning that stasis and/or following a script others wished to author, imploring me to follow, would *absolutely* end in tragedy if it did not offer tangible ameliorative promise on many levels and decisively vibrate inside me in deep truth. Nothing in all the many different modalities I encountered resonated inside me as decisively as the energies of the Casa.

By consistently invoking a contrarian spirit in viewing my challenge, I'd embraced what many could only consider utter nonsense: subscribing to the presence of healing Spirits I could neither see nor truly know from any accepted empirical basis. In this I had simultaneously no choice and every choice in the world, as my free will to choose treatment collided head-on with a conclusive allopathic dead end. What I didn't know at the time was the preordained nature of the odyssey my choices were to set into motion. That realization would only come later as destiny revealed its fuller purpose by exposing me to unimaginable levels of healing. In the meantime I was bull-headed enough to rail against protocols that did not reverberate inside me. At the same time I was open-minded enough to consider stepping entirely outside anything I'd ever known in pursuit of what seemed impossible. No matter the rationale motivating me, I knew I was in for one hell of a ride.

As formidable as is the presence of my discarnate Spirit benefactors to the continuing stability of my symptoms and to my amelioration, it is still up to me whether I engage in or disengage from the mental/emotional reorientation obligatory to recovery. Change takes effort, and in my case, given such a lengthy history of denial and separation from truth, an enormous, concerted effort. My toils have been made immeasurably more meaningful by the sheer number of epiphanies, insights and enlightenment presenting themselves to me, acting in unison as markers in leading me to the right path.

In equal measure, as my *intentions* underwent change and as I drew into consciousness appropriate replacements for old anger, rage and their ancillary emotions, I began to embrace peace, understanding and acceptance. In all of this, I saw Spirit as one *sees* the wind...not directly, face-to-face, but by the way it moved and brought everything around me into crystal clear focus through its vibratory presence. Its energy was always subtle like a whisper, patient, didactic and readily observable once I knew where to look. Its presence continues to lend me the strength to persevere.

• • •

THE STRONGEST MAN I ever knew was my father. Far from being an imposing physical specimen or possessed of the kind of personal charisma that made heads turn whenever he entered the room, Dad demonstrated his real strength...a quiet, stoic resolve...when his first son, my older brother, met his untimely demise two days shy of his nineteenth birthday. My father single-handedly held our family together at the most extraordinarily difficult time we would ever face together. Still in my teen years at the time tragedy struck, I was in awe of his strength. Now, gazing back through the lens of time, I marvel even more at his courage and determination. He modeled perseverance for me in the demonstrative way that would inform the advent of my own crisis almost three decades later, inspiring me to plumb my depths for a similar wellspring of strength and resolve.

Ultimately, I discovered I, too, possessed the stamina required to meet my challenge head-on. To a great extent my odyssey has centered on the discovery of the very same spiritual sinew he first modeled for me. I discovered that, though present inside my core, it lay dormant and untested for so long as to seem all but invisible. It took my years-long struggle with monumental adversity for it to surface and transform my heart from a cell of long-held pain to the rightful vessel of joy and grace, every soul's birthright into completeness.

I've often been asked how I've been able to maintain a decidedly positive, upbeat attitude in the face of an oppressively long, challenging bout with such an unforgiving foe. Early on it was only my game face worn like a mask because I didn't want others to see the true extent of my suffering, having convinced myself that feigning stoicism was preferable to confronting the hidden truth buried deep inside. I concealed myself behind a facade of contrived calm because

I had no desire to confront the authentic source of my suffering and long-held pain. The dichotomy I experienced was simply "What purpose is served by venting my spleen and complaining about my sorry lot in life?" alongside feeling absolutely alone, seemingly headed on a fast one-way ticket right out of this world.

My experience thus far in life had consistently reinforced negating my honest emotions as if doing so would somehow neutralize the mounting grief of an inaccessible heart. A war was being waged between the cultural taboo I'd been raised with, shunning free expression of my feelings and those very same feelings which, having been too long suppressed now finally, vehemently, required their long overdue manifestation. Eventually, my emotional angst would undergo a conversion to true happiness as gratitude and grace supplanted any further need for a mask.

It took ten long years into my trek through illness to truly begin to *know* and express real joy from my heart, not in spite of my diagnosis but precisely owing to it. The linchpin for this change was gratitude. As my journey continued unfolding, I began to see just how fortunate I was to still function at what could only be viewed as a very high level. Not to mention simply being alive in the first place, to experience joy and pain and to learn my lessons. Yet what finally galvanized my gratitude was the realization my healing was taking place from the inside out. When I began to understand what was really happening deep inside, in my very heart, I was overwhelmed with gratefulness. It bears repeating that without the love of those emissaries of light, the Entities of the Casa, I would not be where I am today. They were the very conduit to truth that, in the beginning, I didn't even know I lacked.

Not knowing other than through faith when and how physical amelioration would take place didn't lessen my exuberance at realizing its imminent arrival in the ever expanding *process* of my cure. The prerequisite to deeper levels of healing was exploring what purpose illness served by being here in the first place. I sought congruence between my now informed suffering and the inner transformation toward wholeness enveloping me like a knowing light. What could be learned here? How might I act as a channel for change moving forward?

It became more and more clear to me that the message of the dis-ease I'd manifested was centered in my need to change how I viewed life and how I chose to be in the world. That was the obvious answer, yet an important one to have clear in my mind and newly opening heart. As a journal entry describes, my initial forays inside my self were tentative and laden with anxiety.

Journal entry:

I'm feeling emotionally fragile today...a little door having opened inside where some of the ooze of all these long buried feelings can start seeping out and be accounted for, exposed to the higher purpose of being examined, understood and resolved.

The old me says don't go there...don't open Pandora's box because you really don't want to confront these long bottled-up feelings and emotions. The new me says...and clearly in a stentorian tone...get in there and attend to what hasn't been dealt with before. Open up those abscesses of pain and unhealthy beliefs and drain them of their life-force-sapping energy and replace it all with good, honest expressions of love of self and self-awareness.

And be aware it will not be an easy thing to do, but working on it each time it bubbles to the surface and not shunting it off is the only way it can ever be resolved.

Beyond the archetypal significance, it was not lost on me that my missing voice was the most obvious and profound symptom of not having *spoken* my truth almost from day one. I'd deprived myself of a voice long before illness ever had. That I'd ultimately manifested speechlessness in my physical form was simply the universe supporting my aberrant decision not to honor my truth. By not having given *voice* to my deepest truths...by not having given myself permission to wholly *voice* my spirit...over time the holographic shadow created by dishonoring my soul's truest expression first evidenced itself in my various light bodies before coming to rest in my physical being in the form of an energetic impasse. All illness initially takes form in this way, as an energetic blockage. The only questions are: When will it manifest in the physical body, and Will the afflicted party listen to what it has to say?

Along the way, as I struggled with my lessons, I became aware of a greater good that could be served by my survival, a purpose far removed from just me, me, me. I consulted several other mediums who channeled some very similar information about me and my soul from beyond this plane of existence. I became increasingly aware I was being prepared for my real mission on this earth: helping others heal. This revelation surprised me initially but didn't come as a complete shock.

When I considered I'd spent the previous ten years clawing my way back to the truth, fighting enormous odds against survival, waging battle against considerable personal demons, in the throes of being cured of an incurable disease by elevated spirit Entities, watching as virtually every facet of my life underwent renewal and awakening…it all led seamlessly to the benediction of being in a position to finally give back from the point of having been there, having survived and most importantly having learned. In my heart I felt nothing less would be sufficient. If this were to come to fruition it would involve creating the right atmosphere by deliberately holding the intention in my heart and through a willing receptivity to be guided, not by forcing the issue through the colander of the analytical left brain.

One friend remarked to me I'd earned powerful street credentials: I'd come damn close to the brink of finality and returned a changed man. Through my perilous but purposeful saga I'd been given rare insight into the nature of the soul's purpose in assuming physical form. I'd educated myself in significant ways. True to the revelatory self-examination journaling offered me I'd slowly written myself clear of my demons and into much deeper self-awareness. I'd prayed with deep gratitude, built a now unshakeable faith and found a way to carry on in the face of a steady onslaught of people telling me my dream of a cure was simply a flight from reality: destined to fail not because they didn't want me to succeed in my quest but because the consensus reality they subscribed to informed them this should be so. Yet all of it would mean little if Spirit hadn't decided I could help my fellow man. I'm being groomed for a position from which I can help others. Though I don't yet know what form this will take I know it as surely as my many previous *knowings* have led me to other answers, direction and wisdom. I welcome the opportunity.

I've always had an *awareness* I was meant to do something meaningful in life even during a childhood that while deeply challenging was illuminated by what I now know as my clairsentience. There was a *presence* frequently whispering to me that there was something *more* I was meant to do, something profound. And while I've considered the possibility it was a message preparing me to receive my illness and its attendant lessons, I now feel it was simultaneously informing me of the potential for what could arise out of disease's informed suffering. Growing up, I could never put my finger on what this *knowing* was, nor did I at that time possess the consciousness to be able to fathom its point of origin nor what it was trying to tell me. Yet it was always out there on the edge of what I now know as my beyond-the-five-senses non-rational consciousness quietly lurking, gently but insistently prodding me to listen to its message.

In the course of my ongoing awakening I discovered I was able to *feel* other's emotions on an energetic level. From my earliest childhood I've been alert and hyper-sensitive to the emotional energies around me. In some situations I'm more receptive to this connection than in others. These days I've found it has a lot to do with how centered, focused and still I am within. If I've chosen a judgmental state of mind and heart such a choice blocks me from greater receptivity. Choosing to be *open* to access and "read" what my connectivity picks up is a product of conscious awareness, of placing myself in a state of accessibility. Because I was so hyper-sensitive to such energies I often took on what others were experiencing emotionally in a kind of unconscious osmosis that deeply affected my physical mood and emotional equilibrium.

It's important to note that during my years-long exile from having a heart open and available, I wasn't able to understand or process these vibrations of empathic connectivity with others. I felt them, often deeply, yet the missing element preventing my deeper understanding of how to work with this gift was my own disconnection from heart awareness.

From the very beginning I'd never understood what was happening to me, I had no ready insights into the existence of such energies nor anyone in my life who understood what they signified. Absent any insightful discernment was the compounding effect of a child ill-equipped to explain the tumultuous sensations roiling around inside...all further exacerbated by my near epic disassociation.

For many years prior to my introduction into renewed wholeness I acted as a kind of psychic sponge wicking up the moods of others with vacuum-like efficiency, assuming temperaments and energies not my own...frequently to my detriment. This process was further exacerbated by low self-esteem and an inherent willingness to identify with almost anyone else if it seemed it might bring me closer to my longing for completeness. When at last the pendulum began to swing in the other direction, towards alignment with deeper, richer personal intimacy in the light of self-knowing, I was able to make sense out of years of confusing sensations I'd *felt* all along, without being able to comprehend their significance.

When I was growing up, the adults populating my life frequently chastised me for so freely displaying my emotions, or in the parlance of the time, "wearing my heart on my sleeve." In the 1950's and 1960's of my coming-of-age, real men never showed emotion, instead adhering to an unspoken code that demanded a tough, resilient façade no matter the challenge. It was as much a societal expectation as was wearing a suit and tie to work. While my own father was a very kind man, it became clear to me early on how uncomfortable he was in the presence of emoting by other males...including his sons. Not knowing any other way to be except who I already was, I did my best to hide my true feelings inside. In this way I deepened the already sizeable disenfranchisement from nurture and love I'd first experienced when my mother became emotionally unavailable to me when I was four or five.

I vividly recall being confused and overpowered by the clamorous torrent of feelings threatening to consume me as I grappled with emotions that while often not my own may as well have been for the enormous influence they exerted over me. Unable to moderate their effects nor protect myself from their intensity I was captive to their power. I often didn't know which feeling was my own and which came from someone else close at hand. At last becoming aware of my true identity through the auspices of the awakening self provided a liminal vantage point from which to view this long misunderstood facet of my personal story.

In one transcendent if not long overdue instant it illuminated what had always been occult, concealed beneath decades of shame and derision. I couldn't help noting how entire lives and worldviews are indelibly altered by cues we as malleable youngsters take from our surroundings. Only the plangent urgency of dis-ease tolling deep inside forced me to wake up and abandon the dream state I'd gripped tightly like a security blanket for so long.

Without Spirit blessing me with its loving imprimatur, I know I would've been ineffectual in locating the different levels of consciousness necessary to guide me toward the gradual restoration of homeostasis. I also had to contend with an ego continually telling me this newly discovered gift was all about me and not in service to something much grander. The process of sublimating the center of such formidable power remains a work in progress as I continue learning balance.

Journal entry:

This afternoon I sat "in current" in the operating room at the Casa. As I waited with eyes closed in meditation for Joao-incorporating-the-Entity to enter the room I took stock of how I felt.

The heat from the high sun outside permeated the adobe walls of the room. The temperature in the room steadily increased and even the presence of the industrial sized wall fan whirring madly from its perch was unable to keep the space comfortable.

I realized not only was I feeling the pronounced heat-induced lethargy which has become a constant post-lunch companion on these siesta-perfect afternoons but I was also experiencing something else.

I felt a profound weakness throughout my body which, in times past, I've come to associate with low blood sugar. This potent combination caused me to slump down even farther in my wheelchair and rest my head on an extended arm leaning my cheek on unwillingly straightened fingers as a prop.

When Joao-incorporating-the-Entity entered the room he, the spirit Entity now occupying Joao's body and in complete control of all of its normal functions, announced he was Saint Francis of Assisi, a well known saint and one of the most beloved of the Casa Entities.

There are by various counts between thirty-five and thirty-eight different spirit Entities who at one time or another individually incorporate in the medium Joao's physical form. These Spirits have differing levels of power and specific reasons for incorporating on a particular day. During these bodily "occupations" Joao, the medium, remains in a trance state literally unconscious of what is transpiring all around him.

With my eyes still closed I heard the Entity repeat his name several more times as if to reinforce not only his special presence but as a harbinger of some singular healing to come. With eyes still closed I listened intently as he occupied himself with several people lying on the hospital style gurneys towards the front of the room.

As his voice began to move I realized he was headed towards where I sat in a back corner of the sparsely filled room. My heightened level of awareness was accompanied by a nervous excitement as I wondered what would happen next and to whom. When he moved behind my wheelchair and told my helper to go sit in the front of the room I knew that someone was me.

He started to wheel my chair out from its resting place wedged up against the back bench. When I realized it wasn't moving I checked the handbrakes and released them as he seemed unaware of that need. I entertained the thought while he may be a saint and highly elevated in the realm of Spirit he still needed some assistance with basic mechanical things! This irony struck the humorist in me and except for the always solemn way in which he's received it was all I could do to keep from chuckling at this incongruity.

He summoned a young woman from the front of the room and began demonstrating something on me I didn't fully understand as he was speaking rapidly in hushed tones and, of course, in Portuguese, which at the time I was still learning.

As he laid his hands across my head he explained to this woman the need to "concentrate the energy" and to repeat something "nine times." It was obvious she was a medium he was instructing in the finer nuances of her gift. He alternated between placing his hands and then hers on my head and shoulders. This lasted for more than ten minutes.

During this time I felt different sensations. First I felt shame. Taken out of context that may seem an odd feeling to experience. But in that moment I strongly sensed the direct conduit between myself and Source facilitated by St. Francis' presence and further amplified by the extraordinary spiritual energies present all around us. In that moment I felt an instantaneous need to tell God I was sorry I'd ever doubted His presence as well as the healing process I'm undergoing...a process I enjoy entirely through His beneficence. This emotion was extremely powerful although the entire episode of contrition couldn't have lasted much more than fifteen seconds.

Next I felt a sensation throughout my entire body that can only be defined by saying it was somewhere between a glowing feeling and a humming vibration. As many jumbled thoughts and images raced across my mind and as I sought to quiet my now hyperactive senses I began to feel a great, all pervading peace flood through me.

Then St. Francis was gone as he moved into the adjacent room to assist others. I remember having an odd thought strike me in that moment: Had this all really happened or was it just a dream I'd had, having fallen asleep in a hot, stuffy room during meditation?

I felt as though I'd just returned from some extraordinary place and suddenly was no longer able to quantify what I'd just experienced.

After the session ended one of the Casa mediums approached me saying how incredible it was to have witnessed what had just happened to me. Proof enough.

The ultimate irony is not lost on me. That I could be afflicted with an incurable disease, have everything stripped away that comprised the life I once knew, experience profound physical deterioration, watch as the majority of people I'd once thought of as friends fade from the scene, impotently stand by as my anger, resentment and frustration were further exacerbated by psychological isolation...that all of this could rain down on me and still I could end up thanking each terrible facet of it for how it informed me and opened me to such transformative awakening...this is at very least one of the true miracles I've enjoyed.

Call it a steadily unfolding insight, call it the process I was born to participate in, what remains beyond any attempt at describing it is the purpose it served in illuminating the need for change in my life. Yet it was impossible to find anything even remotely resembling gratitude when I was so buried in challenge and misery that I was blind to any goodness which may have been present.

What appears so obvious now wasn't apparent during the long years spanning my invented consciousness. That's the term I use to describe the false reality I'd constructed in order to adapt the world to my grossly unreal expectations of it. My earliest memories were that something profound was missing from life, although at that stage of my existence this sensation presented itself only as a feeling...a *sensing*...incapable of being articulated into any words I had at the time.

This emotional impression was extremely strong...forceful enough to derail me from the truth. Like a chameleon I learned to adapt myself to perceived threats without being conscious of the reaction such a choice set into motion. My defensive strategy was to erect an exo-skeleton to shield my malnourished heart from the near occasion of hurt in all its myriad forms. By doing so I effectively blocked access to what I needed most...a heart available to give and receive, a vessel open and willing to commune with love.

In that closed off space overflowing with a decades-deep anxiety I housed my fragile emotions in a protected niche, safe from the heartache the world continued flinging my way. The guarded space I'd fabricated was unable to conceal or heal the ponderous extent of my wounding. It sprang into existence as a survival coping skill... grossly ill-suited to any potential for healing and simply an autonomic response to the product of my fears.

Not long after I'd entered this world I stopped knowing what was real and what was merely an invention of my deepest longing for completion. This state of being lasted over forty-five years. The lines between what was real and what I'd invented had blurred sufficiently for me to mistake one for the other. If reality is perception magnified by desire and brought to life by intent, then my view of the world had acute deficiency as its underpinnings. Coming from such gnawing lack, I created a separate reality to provide me with what I wasn't getting from the unacceptable *other* reality. Having constructed my entire life on such shaky footings, there was only one thing that could've happened. And it did.

• • •

WHEN I BECAME conscious I began observing the flow of energy I created and that emanating from others. I made it my obligation to allow and discern when viewing those around me in an attempt to move beyond judgment, something I'd had a long history of succumbing to by taking the easy way out it represented. Gradually I taught myself to redirect my energy from intolerance to acceptance, from anger to understanding, from complaints to gratitude. I felt empowered by the realization that I could heal myself in significant emotional ways as part of a new life practice, thus positively impacting the work the spirit Entities had undertaken on behalf of my cure. In place of pointing my finger at the behavior of others I began examining the ways in which I deprived myself of wholeness. I became an observer of what made me tick in order to better understand what made me sick.

I marveled at what one of my Spirit guides referred to as my "awakening." What he meant by this term was my opening to truth, to emotional integrity, to my own realness. I'm fascinated at how "it" continually informs my mind and heart with insights of growth, healing and transformation. I often experience life in a rarified space charged with purpose and lessons. This sensation is steadily increasing in scope and frequency. Given the presence of all the mundane tasks and dutiful rhythms of my challenged day, it's a welcome, enlightening occurrence to be savored and learned from. In place of shunning awareness I now greet its daily insights into the nature of my being grateful in anticipation of further growth. I now meet head-on challenges I used to flee. I feel the pendulum swinging away from old ways and outdated behaviors. This signals to me that I'm no longer stuck.

Throughout the evolving process of self-discovery I've been struck by the role unseen forces played in my journey. I wondered where acquiescence stopped and trust in all the unknowables began. Were they seamless commodities, conjoined twins, simply congruous parts of a greater whole? Or did they measure the distance between two distinct realities, both separating and connecting humanity from and to the divine? Fact is, they were always present as I struggled with physical and spiritual trials. I'd no sooner concede begrudging defeat on one point or another and there would be this thing called faith once again blossoming deep in my core to buoy up my deflated spirit.

What I was starting to see was an emerging pattern manifest as I began to meet one obstacle after another head-on. For one still not used to self-discernment this new relationship represented a perfect synthesis of lessons coupled with informed choice, as layered in its purpose as it was brilliant in design. Yes, I had great blocks of time in which to ponder the depths of this new life opening up in front of me, intent on teaching me. In this, too, being disabled and incapable of holding a job served a predestined intention. This time I did not turn a deaf ear when it beckoned. My new "job" was to awaken and heal myself through personal growth. Overtime was mandatory.

8

Doing My Promise

THERE IS A certain comfort in fear, a strange contradiction to embracing those things about life that in no way serve our growth but which we cling to anyway because they are known, quantifiable and safe. Most of us remain firmly entrenched in the status quo where old emotional patterns are concerned, stuck in our stubborn ruts, dulled by mindless repetition due to the safety and sameness of their ritual and our adamant avoidance of anything that smacks of change. We want our lives to be patterned and predictable without a hint of anything disruptive. If there's some pain involved, well, isn't that just the price we pay to avoid the spectre of even greater trauma?

I lived just this kind of life, a stickler for the details corroborating the perception that I had all my ducks in a row. I kept busy to keep those monsters lurking just below the surface at bay. In my self-perpetuated little cosmos, emotional integrity was a foreign notion. I'd never thought in terms that would put me in a position of having to deal with my feelings. Instead I maintained a blissful ignorance. When the hammer finally fell, my precious little make-believe world shattered like an eggshell. I scrambled around trying to pick up the pieces but to no avail.

Salvation often comes in unexpected ways. Early on in my diagnosis I was focused on one thing: survival at any cost. In those days following receipt of my death sentence, I barely slept, staggering through the hours as if in a trance. I wore the raiments of fear, saw fear in everything, drank in fear, was consumed by fear. My anxieties were so great that for some years following the "news," I needed someone to stay with me almost around the clock, even though I could still function relatively well on my own. I experienced panic attacks and even bouts of agoraphobia-like symptoms during this fear-besotted hell. I was wildly, madly grasping after any control I could exercise in my life, willing to pay almost any price for the narcotic-like sensation it promised, if only momentarily, to assuage my acute terror. True to my history, I sought out any and all remaining pockets of life where I could maintain a façade of dominion over what was steadily whittling away at me. In that physical space and state of mind, apprehension built on yet more fear all but depriving me of rational thought. The laws of attraction were manifesting precisely what lay in my mind and heart.

Over time, as I became familiar with the "witness" my father's Spirit had spoken of, and let go of my defensive posture, my anxieties slowly began to evaporate. As nature abhors a vacuum, what replaced all that trepidation was a newfound sense of peace and well-being. And while certainly won at great cost, it represented the dawning of a new day in which my spiritual conviction was no longer absent from my life but precisely the motivating principle guiding it.

Journal entry:

As one of my spirit guides offered in response to my interest in knowing what I could do to participate more fully in my healing:

~Pray...pray for help because it is lined up and waiting.

~Change the channel of your heart...open it to such a big size and open it to the suffering of others.

~If you continue to suffer in ignorance you will accomplish nothing.

~There is a lot you haven't learned about why you're ill.

~You need to be obsessed by the love of and compassion for others.

~You experienced a grave trauma when the illness first came on that needs to be resolved.

~We come to this earth to learn about the heart.

~You need to cry from the bottom of the well of emptiness.

It was an extraordinary, profound and deeply emotional channeled session that touched me to my core. It was also a healing gift of love from these Spirits...an insight laden synopsis of what I still need to do in order to aid my cure.

I didn't embrace this guidance until some years afterwards. It took the intervening time to fully realize just what these comments really meant in terms of the responsibility I had to heal myself. Although I felt the imprint of the Spirit's words in my heart and understood them intellectually, I was still so new to the process of assimilating them into daily life in practical ways, I was only able to let them in very slowly, like an intravenous drip...in tiny, measured amounts over a long period of time.

It took a combination of events, continued personal growth and an entirely new perspective based in love, compassion and forgiveness for me to be able to absorb and implement my Spirit guide's teaching. I'd operated for so long from a mindset that said "If I'm not sick, then I must be well," that I wasn't able to conceptualize the notion that the absence of illness did not automatically dictate the presence of wellness. Ironically, my father used to frequently quote from M. Scott Peck's book "The Road Less Traveled" regarding this very concept. It took a Spirit guide speaking directly to me in order for me to realize the gravity of my wrong thinking.

I thought back to the 70's when Carlos Castaneda's books first came within my radar. I recalled my astonishment at reading about shamans, nahuals, portals to separate realities and the beings who inhabited such realms. While these flights into other worlds made for compelling reading, Castaneda's journeys read like some fantastic spiritual fiction utterly devoid of any connectivity to my frame of reference: singular, exotic and surreal.

Suddenly, I found myself smack dab in the middle of a similar adventure. Only the experiential sojourn was my own, authored by my keen interest in healing modalities outside accepted "reality." I'd discovered I could enter and exit alternate levels of reality readily and almost effortlessly. And far from being escapes into mind-numbing daydreams, these were active, working expeditions into a sacred arena containing astonishing information readily available to me, the fledgling numenaut.

I found it impossible to articulate what I was experiencing... from Spirit interventions to my ever increasing "knowings"...in the analytical left-brain manner I was accustomed to using. Even early on in my shamanic journeys, I'd moved beyond the limitations of the five senses to a place of deepening, intuitive knowing. In this realm there didn't seem to be any constraints to accessing whatever information I needed to fulfill my hunger for answers, direction and guidance. It was one thing to receive direct communication from discarnate Spirits but a wholly unique experience to be able to tap into a borderless repository that held images of my past lives, where I could converse with souls I'd interacted with then, and where I could receive vital insights that exerted a dramatic impact on my current journey.

I pondered whether the ethereal connectivity I enjoyed was the product of wisdom contained within my own higher self or sprang from some vast store of all the information that had ever existed, like the Akashic records. Or did it emanate from some symbiotic, peri-spiritual connection between the two? For some time now I'd felt my intuitive powers growing and expanding to where it was no longer appropriate to limit myself to anything resembling a traditional interpretation of reality. Now my burgeoning new consciousness had to make room for those empathic facets of my persona that claimed greater authenticity, power and purpose than anything which had come before.

Journal entry:

I was invited to go to the Entity's sacred waterfall the other day along with a group of fifteen men, including two others wheelchair-bound like myself. This journey has eluded me all the years I've been coming to the Casa de Dom Inacio because the terrain doesn't lend itself to handicapped accessibility. Bouyed by the good intentions and brute strength of all present I was finally able to access the extraordinary energy in this special place.

Recently they'd widened the path and rebuilt the bridges so that this was the first time in the more than thirty years the Casa has been in existence that those confined to wheelchairs were able to successfully complete the trek down to the falls. I was very pleased to be at the vanguard of this newly accessible sacred spot.

The approach was a very steep, gravelly path reminiscent of an Olympic ski jump in its ladle-like swoop and curve. With a single guide wire strung through successive wooden posts anchored in concrete on the edge separating the path from a precipitous drop-off, it would be touchy going for even the sturdy of limb.

The women in the group had gone first as the sexes aren't allowed by the Entity to commingle at this site. No photographs or recordings of any sort are permitted in deference to its sacred nature. Three or four men braced each of our wheelchairs and slowly edged them down the slope, seeking purchase in loose soil that was hostile to their constantly braking mission.

Finally, we found ourselves on more level ground and rolled along toward the first of two small, narrow-width bridges over several chasms and water-fed canyons. After we'd negotiated the first one we came to a slight rise and, gaining the crest, peered down into a cavernous depression hollowed out of the sparsely forested terrain.

As we crossed a second bridge we gazed into a foliage-darkened lair and spotted the modest waterfall cascading over a stone shelf and down some ten feet to a holding pool below where the water churned and roiled with the impact of its fall. We noted how treacherous it would be for anyone with the slightest physical infirmity to attempt an ascent up to the base of the fall. The water-smoothed stones, which successively but irregularly tiered upward from this point, seemed impassable by anyone less than sure-footed.

When it came my turn to be carried up to the site of what I considered a baptism of renewal, I said a short prayer invoking the Entities who were present and gave myself over to trust and faith in my handlers.

My assistant for all these past months, a man of considerable physical strength, hoisted me up out of my wheelchair and onto his shoulder in one fluid motion. The fact that I was six inches taller and must've outweighed him by thirty pounds seemed of little concern to him. Braced by many hands pushing against my tall but bent-over frame, we began the climb. My helper slipped several times but quickly found his footing again and with many outstretched limbs vying to support my body, in a matter of moments we'd completed the climb.

After standing me upright like a fencepost at the base of the waterfall, my helper managed to place my feet next to one another and at my signal tipped me under the falling water. It was chilly but refreshing, especially on a warm day when the temperature must've been eighty-five plus. In the sacred grotto surrounded by vegetation, with steep embankments on every side, the cold torrent was invigorating. I had my helper tip me under five times before I felt my shocked nervous system and muscles had had enough. The descent went off without a hitch, and I was soon back in my chair where I took the opportunity to examine the faces of my compatriots.

We represented England, Israel, Brazil, Ireland and the United States. We were Christians, Jews, Anglicans, Hare Krishnas, Spiritists, and those without any formal religious ties. Our ages ranged from nineteen to close to seventy-five. The camaraderie in our group was palpable even though many of us had only seen each other in passing at the Casa. The common bond we shared was our desire to heal and to access the extraordinary spiritual gifts found by stepping under an ordinary looking waterfall.

The topography where the Casa de Dom Inacio is situated is butte-like in that it occupies a flat shelf of land on top of a nondescript promontory at the far terminus of one side of the town of Abadiania. From the crown of this butte one can gaze for miles in three directions at the gently sloping patchwork of crops, scrub vegetation and second growth timber, lines of sight broken only by modest, tile-roofed adobe houses which seem to pop up out of the rolling earth like Lilliputian cottages against the sheer enormity of land and sky.

The small, ordinary-looking waterfall came out of the same quartz crystal-rich hill where the Casa is situated providing enormous spiritual energies, with the water acting as a naturally conductive medium. I'd been told by all who'd been under the falls that it'd changed them in some way although it was often difficult for them to articulate precisely how. Past being jolted by the cold blasts of water pouring down over me and by anecdotal evidence of its transformative powers, I hadn't felt anything unusual.

As I sat quietly after my bracing shower I closed my eyes and again connected with the Entities, praying to be open to this experience and take away some truth, some teaching from this special place.

When I first noticed a change in my body, I was sitting down in the taxi that would take us up the steep dirt road from the waterfall back to our inn. Initially it felt like a subtle tingling throughout my body, which I assumed was due to the effects of cold, wet shorts and the goosebump-laden skin they covered meeting hot, dry air.

However, as we neared our destination some three kilometers away, it continued to build into a sensation of absolute aliveness, as though I'd been hooked up to a massive power grid, which sent wave upon wave of energy into every cell and molecule in my body.

Not being in possession of an intelligible speaking voice, I was forced to keep my excitement and thoughts about what I was experiencing to myself. What a powerful, transcendent and astonishing feeling! What was this sensation that threatened to turn me into an electrical substation?

As I considered various possibilities, it came to me in a flash: this was simply but powerfully the manifestation of what I'd asked the Entities to help me open to. It was love. But not as I was used to experiencing it.

This was L-O-V-E, without qualifiers, sans judgments, devoid of human urge, need and want, creating a state of exquisite, absolute bliss. It was as close as I've ever been to ecstasy. My physical body felt as though, in having been ushered into this state of delight, it was weightless, without concerns, at unconditional peace. In that moment I experienced what it meant to be connected to the purity of Source.

I felt the overpowering need to smile with boundless joy. I felt so blissful I even hugged the startled kitchen worker who'd brought me coconut water as I started to eat my lunch back at the pousada. I sat with this sensation, observing it, stunned by its power and transformed by its presence, awash in wonder and veneration at being given this transcendent blessing.

Slowly, in a fashion similar to how I feel as the energy gradually fades at the end of meditations while I'm sitting in current, I noticed the blessed sensation vanishing from my body while still remaining an intense focus of my awareness.

On relating this seminal experience to a friend, he remarked, "... it seems you've been touched by the Holy Spirit." I couldn't argue with his interpretation. I had been touched. It was further dramatic proof I was on the right track in my return from spiritual deprivation. While I'd already experienced much in the way of interaction with Spirit-fomented phenomena, this exceptional instance proved vital in helping me graduate into the next level of awareness.

My life had been a lot like the Entity's waterfall: rushing headlong over one precipice after another only to crash on the rocks below, propelled by an inner, intransigent force, oblivious to the detritus it churned up along the way. My perceived deficiencies always goaded me forward as if hurrying up my pace could in some way imbue my life with added substance or purpose, if not also make up for lost time. Though seldom fueled by a conscious pattern of choice,

I didn't let that stop my resolute impetus...my determined uncon-sciousness...from advancing at a dizzying pace. My mind's clamor-ing for still more speed clouded an inner wisdom, whose existence I could hardly have suspected less, an inner discernment that knew the extent of the problem concealed by decades of denial.

After all the time I've spent at the sacred healing site in Brazil one thing has become certain in my mind and heart. The spiritual evolution I'm undergoing operates on levels both subtle and dramatic. Though my analyzing, questioning, curious mind always seeks answers and reasons, my heart is learning to surrender to a far greater presence. The predestined merger of my soul and body into this incarnation points me in the direction of those lessons best suited to growth.

What began as my frenetic need to heal my body *at any cost* has been subtly transformed into healing my spirit first. The rest will follow. Of that I remain confident, if not always patient. After repeatedly being counseled by the Entities that I was getting bet-ter, I finally acknowledged their comments. Granted such gifts as experiencing the bliss of unqualified love at the waterfall, my heart finally opened to receive their pre-eminent sustenance, and I *felt* for the first time love in its purest form. I discovered I'd been operating with a woefully incomplete definition of what the words *love* and *healing* really mean. Added to which, an unavail-able heart meant I couldn't be open to the miracle unfolding right in front of me.

When at last my blinders came off, I was able to see my miracle manifesting before my eyes. And even though it's difficult for me to adequately relate the sheer enormity of this experience, I'm con-vinced that with time it will all make perfect sense as dramatic heal-ing becomes the rule and no longer the exception. It is happening right now. I am living proof.

• • •

As I TREKKED deeper into the territory of dis-ease I witnessed a curi-ous dichotomy taking shape. On one hand, as the years and my gradual bodily enfeeblement progressed...albeit at a snail's pace...I was forced to become increasingly consumed with coordinating my care and deal with the resultant bustle of activity swirling all around me. This necessity juxtaposed against the sense of almost complete isolation from the deep, meaningful relationships I yearned for. I gradually learned the benefit of forging ahead into this not unfamiliar reclusiveness because I knew that what awaited my arrival *must* be the sacrament of insight revealed from within that silent locale.

I discovered inside such a calm, holy space as this lay expression without need for words, an evolved language of sensing, complete and perfect in what can never be articulated, which I could access... along with its profound blessings...if I was willing to be tutored. I discovered in the presence of frustration an invitation to a deeper acceptance of patience, grounded in a categorical letting go. Though I couldn't quantify this *language* I "knew" it was knowledge worth gaining.

The primary rhetorical question generated by my claim of miracles is, What proof do I have I'm being cured? After all, I've no written statement from the spirit Entities, no testament to a panacea-in-progress, no externally quantifiable evidence in my physical organism to support the assertion I'm on the mend. Other than the glaringly obvious fact that I've far outlasted my death sentence while receiving marked amelioration many times over the unprecedented span of time since diagnosis. Aside from the Entity's oft repeated admonition, "You are improving and you will continue to improve," I have just one validation buoying my trust in what I can never fully comprehend: faith-this and a marked increase in conscious awareness as my heart slowly emerged from its self-imposed exile.

If I am being cured, why haven't my symptoms begun receding? After all, I was first told in September 1998 I would be cured. It was explained I'd need to muster patience and faith along the way for however long my healing might take, without my being given an end date when at last I'd find myself delivered to the doorstep of health. I'm careful not to say "returned" to health because in truth I wasn't living in a state of wellness and equilibrium to begin with. I had no desire to return to such imbalance. This alone compelled me to work very hard on my issues once I finally woke up.

Later, as I again sought out an audience with the Entity in order to clarify *when* I could expect to be cured he'd responded with the ambiguous reply, "There isn't a day in which it will be done." I was further informed that the discarnate spirit Entities coordinating treatments in service to my blossoming cure were providing me everything I required to effect physical rejuvenation.

I *felt* many of those around me wondering if I'd swung so far away from acknowledgment of my original diagnosis that I was now ready to believe that those unseen could accomplish a seemingly impossible feat. I repeatedly asked myself if I'd so distanced myself from consensus reality I was ready to accept the utterly implausible? I had to answer this koan-like question for myself, absent the almost unilateral contrary opinions of those occupying my life. The answer couldn't be found in my mind but only in my heart. It wouldn't arrive on the chariot of rational thought. It had to come on the wings of the heart's own intelligence. I chose to move forward into the unknown, in place of settling for stasis or adopting the finality staunchly adhered to by western medicine. Instead, I relied on the often ambiguous statements of Spirit and on my own burgeoning confidence in a divine design.

This was part of the pact I'd negotiated in-between incarnations, while on the other side of the great curtain. It became apparent that an integral part of my lesson was faith itself, trusting myself to faith in a process never clearly spelled out, developing faith in the wisdom contained in my heart, by opening that vessel to the light of its true purpose. In accordance with the wisdom of my Spirit benefactors, providing me a precise timeline for rejuvenation might only allow me to idly sit back and await my cure, in place of exerting myself through trial and error to achieve healing. They knew me better than I knew myself. Now they were asking me to turn that dynamic around so that "witnessing" my actions, thoughts and emotions and taking the necessary steps to change what required changing would replace the blindness I'd allowed to envelop me my entire life.

Each of us comes into physical form with a specific mission imprinted in our souls. Each of us makes a pact, a sacred promise, to accomplish certain goals in this life. These agreements are made in the company of our spiritual board of trustees: those guides, mentors and angels charged with the duty of ushering our souls along their path of growth. We execute such contracts between our souls and Source as a way of demarcating precise intentions for the new incarnation we are about to enter.

Our "trustees" act as sounding boards for our ideas and the lessons we seek to master by once again assuming flesh and blood form. The final choices as to the instruction we seek by accomplishing these goals and re-entering dense physical form remain our responsibility. In making our promise while still in the realm of Spirit, we're asked to forget our original identities on entering this life along with the contracts we forge with other souls who accompany us into this world. This *forgetting* allows us a clean slate from which to connect with the experiences in life best suited to fulfilling our individual mission and completing our vow untainted by the unfair advantage of prior knowledge. Through the exercise of free will, the choices we make can overwhelm us with misery if we embrace the world's many illusions. Or they can serve as a reconnection to our real identities by allowing elements of our essential truth to pass through the veil to inspire and inform us.

The pain of loss I'd experienced in childhood when I'd made the decision to shutter my heart re-emerged within the contours of my present-day challenge, the lesson returning to test my readiness to learn what it had always sought to teach. Bolstered by the gradual erosion of my stubborn defensiveness and buoyed by the steady infusion of transcendent phenomena inviting their way into my life, I began to apprehend the lesson I was being shown. Fulfilled by Spirit embracing me at every turn, supporting my right choices, I at last began to comprehend what I'd asked myself to do in this life.

The feeling of abandonment that consumed every aspect of my early self was so disorienting I lost my way in life. That I felt compelled to interpret in the way I did such a disturbing withdrawal of affection previously so freely dispensed was a reaction to having no other apparent choices. It was desperate, immediate and lasting. I developed a stubborn will, non-pareil, an epic refusal to do anything more than defend myself against the pain of further loss. The fear it promulgated invested me with only one desire: *never allow this to happen again.*

In the present moment I continue grappling with issues of abandonment and its lackey, fear. The difference now is that I'm better equipped to deal with it for I'm much stronger emotionally, aware that fear can only be dealt with and diffused by love, not by creating yet another layer of dread. With all the physical challenges of relative immobility, old, deeply ingrained fears continue lingering just below the surface poised to quickly rise up cued by any lapse in vigilance to the awareness I refused to acknowledge for decades. In the last analysis, the greater struggle lies in growing my self-discipline so that challenge and its intrusive energies can be systematically chastened by coming from a calm place of heart.

As we grow up we're presented with many opportunities to learn about discipline and setting personal boundaries. Parents, teachers and other authority figures continually reinforce certain standards of appropriate behavior. Yet if you imagine your life populated solely by lack and view your condition as governed by fear's disequilibrium you fail to locate your center within. The result is that societal signals don't filter through your defenses and register their impressions in the same way they would if your edges were well-drawn and your sense of self whole and uncompromised by constant apprehension.

As a way of coping with not being grounded, you create a universe that gives you what's missing in the greater, generally-agreed-upon reality. But without clearly defined limits, the lines between what's acceptable and what isn't blur. You fail to replace what's missing because what springs from lack of abundance can only be more of the same. You hastily fill in the blank spots in your contrived reality, modifying the unacceptable to fit the dream you'd rather live, but living from expectation doesn't address the truth of who you are, nor the actuality of your surroundings.

By harvesting our interpretation of reality from thoughts not aligned with a clear sense of truth and self grounded in an open heart, we fail to find our rightful course in life. Our passage through existence is thus compromised by the nagging sensation that something indispensable is missing. We find our reason for being forsaken by a lack of that undefinable substance animating our very existence. Although we may keenly *feel* this essence in the pit of our being, we never seem able to grasp and know it. Filled instead with feelings of mediocrity and even futility, we grope for meaning by pursuing *things.* We imbue these substitute objects with great longing, eager to stem the tide of our emotional poverty. To our dismay they're never able to provide the lasting content we pine for because we've confused material content with spiritual purpose. Our minds can only imagine into existence what our hearts feel. In this way the type and quality of our emotions dictate whether we're destined to create a life of meaning or a life of discontent.

• • •

THE EVOLUTIONARY PROCESS of connecting directly with the mystical was happening to more and more people I met. What I witnessed was a profound transformation taking shape on a global scale. I say global, because during my repeated lengthy stays in Abadiania while attending the Casa de Dom Inacio, I had occasion to meet individuals from every part of the world. While many were already spiritually aware, there were an equal number without any attunement to such matters. Like me, they had come solely as a last resort for physical, emotional, psychological or spiritual amelioration. What was common to almost everyone was acceptance of what was alternately described as God, the Creator, Source, All that Is, or, as I've often heard the Entity proclaim when describing God, "the grand architect of the universe."

Invoking assistance from the realm of Spirit benefits each of us in accessing the powerful current of transformation now manifesting on earth. Many of us have experienced this energetic shift in profound ways. Once your awareness to this phenomenon is heightened, the evidence of its startling power becomes compelling. Through prayer I'd discovered a vehicle capable of connecting me with formidable help, eager to shepherd me in my journey while acting as a lodestar to light my chosen path.

I felt strongly that if I failed to rely on this emerging sentient awareness, doing so would give rise to a climate of contraction instead of expansion. In my own journey of healing the peril in such inaction lay in propagating the same spiritual stasis I was now laboring so earnestly to move beyond. Embracing the place and purpose of this new self-examination in the continuum of the soul's destiny meant stepping away from familiar terrain in search of that which I'd discovered has no ready vocabulary. I already had one foot in the pond. It was time to either sink or swim.

My ongoing exposure to alternate levels of reality demonstrated just how much more there was to the "me" I'd always defined through the narrow aperture of consensus thinking. In subscribing to the patterned behavior I'd wicked up along the way, I'd lost touch with my uniqueness. In my specific case it all came down to one thing: expanding the definition of myself in order to discover my authentic personal power.

The shamans and medicine men have known about this kind of power for a very long time. Traditional religion has known of it too and its enormous potential to subvert their message of reliance on man-made orthodoxy. I have extensive personal experience with dogmas purporting to be "the sole truth," having observed and lived first-hand their stultifying effect on my right to choose what to believe.

When I discovered reality beyond the five senses, I opened myself up to a heightened understanding of the true extent of my personal power, a nascent force in the heart that gravitates outward, touching everything with authenticity. Becoming authentic means being factual, authoritative and honest. Entering this truth-filled domain, one comprehends the extent to which a very personal relationship with Source is possible. Integral to comprehending Source, at least to the extent humanly possible, is reacquainting the self with the God-I-am within, the indwelling divinity located deep in the core of one's heart.

An especially startling example of my latent etheric connectivity occurred six months after learning I had a terminal illness. I was traveling in France on what I then thought would be my final trip to Europe...or anywhere else for that matter. It happened while visiting the vast ossuary at Verduns, the site of enormous casualties during WWI. As I entered the building I experienced a very unusual *sensation*. I found myself in the tall arching vault of the battleground mausoleum. An atmosphere of profound heaviness hung suspended in the air as if some ponderous invisible cloud had settled into the marble-clad space, its palpable weight pressing down on me. In that grand, solemn room I felt as if I'd suddenly added two hundred pounds of extra weight to my frame.

I initially dismissed this odd feeling as a consequence of the tiring and disruptive nature of being on the go, as I tried to jam in one more historical site to an already overflowing travel itinerary. Yet after processing this *feeling* over the span of fifteen to twenty minutes, I intuitively discovered the source. In the core of my being I felt the burden of the men who'd died in battle, whose souls were still earthbound, trapped in-between the realm of Spirit and the world of the living, unable to move on to the next phase of their souls' journeys. It marked the first time I'd felt with such remarkable force in my physical and energy bodies the overwhelming psychic weight of so much misery.

While their bones lay interred in the many niches that ran the length of the enormous burial chamber, it was the anguish of their soul's confinement to the earth plane, their inability to move on, which I *felt* deep within the core of my empathic being, a torment that literally bowed my shoulders with its sheer oppressive density. It's important to understand that this sensation wasn't simply my feelings of sadness at the carnage and loss of life that had transpired at this site. For while that was certainly the case what I was experiencing wasn't the interplay of history and emotion, but rather a far more profound and direct *visceral* connection with the presence of a condensed soul energy so powerful and so profoundly deep in misery it threatened to overwhelm my sensitivities with its collective mournful weight.

It was only after some years passed and I'd been repeatedly exposed to direct contact with discarnate Spirits and alternate levels of reality (both while at the Casa de Dom Inacio and in my other spiritual forays) that I'd fully comprehend what I'd experienced that afternoon. I came to a fuller appreciation for the fact that I was a *medium*, naturally imbued with certain psychic gifts, which allowed me access to sensations emanating from other planes of existence, realities both separate from and overlapping our own. In arriving at this insight, I developed a new appreciation for the *significance* of the plight of these souls and for my newly emerging empathic gift, which allowed me to sense their pained earthbound presence in such compelling fashion.

Journal entry:

I had an unusual experience while meditating in the medium's room at the casa last week. I was in a particularly deep state of meditation during the morning session...a state where I'd gotten comfortable in my wheelchair, had successfully quieted my mind and focused my attention on my breathing. In these still rare circumstances when everything seems to work I enter a trance-like state, deep within myself.

Behind me and off to one side a person was moaning and softly crying as if she was in pain. I've heard these sounds many times before in the Casa and hearing it then held no particular significance for me for I've come to understand it's part of that individual's necessary spiritual purge in order to grow.

Suddenly, I began to experience an odd sensation throughout my own physical form, a feeling of tremendous heaviness, as if my body weight had suddenly tripled, accompanied by a nauseated feeling.

This lasted ten or fifteen seconds, then I felt the overwhelming urge to flee the room, a panic washing over me in wave after intense wave. I remembered hearing in my mind the distinct, calming words "this too shall pass...be with the feeling, John, and see where it takes you." While I literally "felt" this message course throughout my being I couldn't tell whether it came from me or arrived from an outside force. I sat in the midst of this sensation and as quickly as it appeared it receded.

I've mulled over this experience for the past week and have come to several conclusions based on my intuition. That the panic-like attack happened in the Casa seems odd as I've never had anything remotely similar to this take place there before. My sense is I may have channeled an energy due to my profoundly deep state of meditation. Or, possibly, an energy passed through me for some unknown but purposeful reason due to my receptivity as a medium of transport.

Yet, as I strictly adhere to the warnings to keep my eyes shut for the entire session (opening one's eyes breaks the current and makes one more receptive to receiving negative energies), I don't know how I could have been a vehicle for this singular experience other than as a consequence of my mediumship.

Another possibility is the feelings I experienced were my physical body's manifestation of some specific work the Entities were doing in my spiritual body. As I've been working hard on my fears lately it may have been fear itself exiting my system.

Update: I've now learned some two weeks later that when the Entity is doing physical surgeries in the other room, often the medium who's most receptive to conducting the special energy being generated will experience some of the physical manifestations of the surgery, at times feeling nausea, various pains or the same "heaviness" I experienced.

I believe one of the reasons I'm now seated in the medium's room along with receiving the special energies that are literally conducted into this space by all present is now I'm also giving these energies to others inside the Casa's three principal rooms by a combination of my mediumship, my desire and intent to do so, coupled with the Entity's manipulation and use of the energy.

I feel I'm being assisted in becoming a better medium, one who can contribute more to the dissemination and conducting of this mighty healing energy.

In all of this profound, mysterious new way of seeing beyond accepted "reality," I came to the process as a child might: with openness, innocence and completely devoid of guile. I came to it as a martyr prepared to sacrifice my "before-ness" for a chance at salvation that, initially, was only concerned with having my physical body survive. I walked through a portal of transmogrification, altering virtually everything in my worldview. How does one describe such life-changing experiences? For one who's continually fascinated by words, I feel ill-equipped to properly honor my rite of passage.

I came to this loving, guiding, infinitely patient energy with wonder. If I felt any momentary disappointment, it was due to my own unreasonable expectations carried over from before. As I surrendered more and more to That Which Knows All I began to harmonize energetically with the greatest truth of all: Love. I'd spent so many years denying my heart's natural rhythms that from the time I first decided to try and heal myself until I freely forgave, let go of pent-up anger and watched as my heart finally started to open, a decade had come and gone. And for all my reluctance to change, now overcome by my concerted efforts to grow further, I've only just begun my work.

In this process of healing self, I'd become a spiritual adventurer trekking through uncharted landscapes in search of any experience capable of placing me in contact with Spirit, guidance and insight. I had enormous difficulty walking but discovered a way to move effortlessly across time and space...assuming they even existed in the first place...to connect with other levels of consciousness. I arrived at a point where I felt no fear in stepping into these new realities. While I certainly wondered where they'd take me, still, at a place deep within my being, I felt the truth of their existence resonate confidently inside, allaying any semblance of misgiving.

There were many contradictions within my daily existence. With so many disparate skeins of my old self insistently vying for a voice, for continuance however inappropriate in the desire to remain unchanged, the process of ushering in transformation on so many fronts seemed Promethean. In addition to which, favorable outcomes were always tempered by Sisyphean attempts to effect lasting betterment as my fervent endeavors met the stultifying resistance of long-held habits.

During this time I chuckled to myself as I was reminded of a quote from John Muir which humorously summed up my existence: "...we are in no danger of being called on to endure one dull moment."

9

Lessons from Spirit

WHAT HAS ILLNESS taught me? Once I began listening to its incessant chorus it demonstrated the absolute need for living a conscious life. It taught me that absent its pain-filled presence I would've continued operating from lack, fear and incompleteness. It showed me that evolving means remaining continually vigilant about how I process my emotions. It also validated the sanctity of my having emotions in the first place, putting me in touch with my heart for the very first time from within a place of absolute truth. It presented me with ways to disagree with others' opinions while learning how not to charge my thoughts with anger, resentment or disrespect for their choices. It persuaded me to value others' sovereign state of individuality by loosening the grip of my expectations. It taught me to cry with empathy and compassion for the enormity of people's pain while understanding their absolute spiritual need to manifest suffering in the first place. It exhibited before my astonished eyes the dramatic ways discarnate Spirits actively intervene in our lives to help guide us through our trials here on this plane of existence, our earth school. The magnificent light-filled energies of the Casa provided an environment of absolute safety in which I could at last open my heart and have it cleansed with love and peace while I gradually learned a new way of being.

On a practical level, as I implemented these new models for thinking and feeling based on techniques I'd acquired during my apprenticeship to all things spiritual, my life underwent a powerful transformation. I'd learned about the energies driving the formidable engines powering my life and how to manage them. I'd taught myself to breathe deeply from my center and relax my hara. I acquired skill in blocking negative vibrations from adversely impacting my emotional center. I put tremendous effort into dismantling old, inappropriate behaviors and the thoughts fueling them. I passionately adhered to a regimen aimed at retooling substantial parts of myself because I was sick of being sick.

All these transformative *insights* were provided without psychotherapy or counselors, without medication or standard therapeutic modalities. They came to me solely through the intercession of elevated Spirit beings, as a consequence of my soul's anguished plea for help. They arrived with the tacit understanding that I *must* open my heart and mind to accept love, truth and light. I *must* forsake fear and cleanse my logjammed heart of all its impurities. No one but myself was responsible for completing this work. It meant nothing less than keeping my sacred promise. I was reminded of the Entity's matter-of-fact response to one of my questions: "What can I do to help my healing?" He'd responded: "I am providing you with everything you need." Only much later would these few words resonate with their full meaning and I would begin to see the real extent of his giving.

I've slowly grown beyond the almost narcotic-like need to return to a robust, pre-disease state knowing as I now do that healing my spirit and soul must be my primary focus. The nexus connecting all points of healing is the heart. That's where my energetic intentions must be fixed. I've progressed to the understanding that by helping others heal I also heal myself. Stepping away from yourself to hold compassion for others creates an energetic matrix, which not only feeds the recipient of your loving intention but your own center as well. It's such a simple notion in theory. Yet, with a core distressed by years of remoteness and all but shut to honest emotion, you neither see nor understand what for you remains an unapproachable dream. The moment you waken into consciousness, you step out of what you've allowed to define your confinement. The moment apprehension is given its marching orders love floods in to fill the vacant roost.

While the lessons presented to me concerning the heart continued unabated, similarly other numinous phenomena revealing their presence to me showed no signs of lessening in frequency nor diminishing in impact. I had ample opportunity to marvel at some of these ongoing lessons. What follows is a dramatic example of just such a teaching.

Journal entry:

I was intently focused on a likeness of the Blessed Virgin affixed to a devotional candle on a small altar containing two bottles of Daime. I was praying to her, thanking her for the beautiful energy of the Santo Daime "work," which having grown steadily over the previous hours was now poised to finish. Already the eight of us gathered in Paul and Caroline's* (pseudonyms used out of respect for privacy) cozy home had witnessed an awe-inspiring display of the presence and power of Spirit.

One of the five women participating in the "work," a gifted medium, had incorporated a very powerful nature Spirit named Jeruma. The Spirit entity occupied the body of a pleasant looking woman with Asian features. When the entity assumed control of this woman's physical form, she shook and noticeably contorted. The medium's eyes went from being full of life to sitting in shrunken sockets, darkening to deep brown muddy pools.

Witnessing the immediate physical transformation in the woman's facial features was as powerful as the realization that what now occupied her form was an ancient spiritual being come to impart much sought-after wisdom. These were now eyes that didn't see in the normal sense of sight. They'd been transformed into bottomless pools that saw what human beings never see.

With the entity now directly in front of my wheelchair, I couldn't help but marvel at the transformation from human being to Spirit entity now temporarily incorporated in physical form. I wondered in that instant why I wasn't frightened by what others would consider a scary wraith, standing not four feet away. I remember thinking I'd seen similar transformations many times before and had grown accustomed to the process.

In addition, the all-pervading presence of love was such a strong and palpable force in the room, it provided even more assurance that the phenomenon, while clearly outside the boundaries of consensus reality, nonetheless was a normal occurrence for anyone at all in touch with Spiritism's vital bridge between this world and realms beyond.

The entity spent a lot of time continuously snapping its fingers in front of various places on my body and bending and twisting in front of me. It spoke with an odd cadence and in a muffled way, as if speaking through heavy fabric, which made understanding it a difficult proposition. I was familiar with the finger-snapping technique as a device used by some mediums to keep their connection with spiritual energies strong.

Later, Caroline, an experienced "madrinha" in Daimista circles, would tell me it was very unusual to see an entity this elevated in the pantheon of Spirit show up at anything other than a large Santo Daime "work" where the accumulated energies of all the participants is so much more powerful. She explained it was equally unusual to see an entity spend so much time working on one person.

Caroline told me the entity said I was very weak and instructed the others involved in the "current" to send me energy. It also stated I was to bathe from the neck down with water containing three special Amazonian herbs that Caroline had in her collection. Like the work the entity had done to remove negative energies lingering in my etheric body, its advice for taking the herbal bath had to do with further cleansing. Paul explained that whenever one attends spiritual healing work in any setting, one can attract discarnate Spirits drawn to the light of truth present in such a place. While normally well-intentioned, these Spirits often carry negative energies that need to be removed if they become attached to one's energy field.

During this part of the small Santo Daime "work," I felt very connected to the energy of love found in the "current" generated by the participants. I expressed my gratitude to the Virgin Mother over and over again in silent prayer.

Acting as the "madrinha" or godmother in the "work," Caroline had the responsibility to call for the Daime to be drunk as well as to choose what prayers and songs would be recited and sung.

When Paul approached me with the bottle of Daime, I made a sign with my hand to say, "Yes, a little please." Paul reverently poured the Daime into a small communal glass and handed it to me. Even though the first glassful had been as bitter and earthy tasting as anything I could imagine, I decided to drink it again, as it seemed a small inconvenience to bear in order to expose myself to spiritual insight. With small sips and accompanying grimaces I slowly found the bottom of the glass. My swallowing limitations wouldn't allow me to mimic the others in downing the drink with one grand motion.

The Daime is ayahuasca, a combination of the product of two plants found in the Amazon. They have no effect if ingested individually. Yet when combined in the correct proportions they're transformed into a powerful entheogen, a psychotropic powerhouse allowing the recipient to gain passage into the astral plane by acting as a spiritual vehicle to higher guidance. They act in tandem to bypass the blood-brain barrier and create a means to unleash a naturally occurring chemical in the pituitary gland called DMT, known as the "Spirit molecule."

I knew this going into my first "work," but I still felt fear wash over me, from the thought of entering an unknown place and possibly losing control in a process I wasn't familiar with. Except for having read one book on the subject and having heard Paul describe the process in a non-proselytizing manner I was a neophyte, a spiritual kindergartner.

Though I've spent countless hours accessing Spirit, my God consciousness, I'd never entered a drug-altered state to attempt a connection with guidance from beyond. I tried to set aside my fear and offered a prayer asking to be shown what I needed most.

From the first glass of Daime, I had a blissful sensation of love, which left me feeling deeply connected to the sacred energy of the "work." Having drunk the second glass, I tried to wait without expectation for whatever sensations, insights or experiences might come. I still hadn't sensed any discernible change in consciousness other than a mild disorientation, a kind of detached and spacey sensation in my mind when the "work" came to an end. During this time I'd had visions of geometric shapes…quite intricate and beautiful… flow through my mind.

After the "work" came to a close, Caroline asked us to come and enjoy soup and bread. Not having had dinner due to wanting to keep from vomiting (a normal side effect of taking Daime) I now felt the need to put something in my stomach. I rolled my wheelchair around in a circle and entered the kitchen where one of the participants from the "work" dished me up some food.

It was then nearing 1a.m. and I was tired, buzzed from the Daime and the energy of the "work" and hungry. As I ate, not fifteen minutes had gone by when I suddenly began feeling very disoriented. I broke out in a drenching, clammy sweat, my vision blurred; my breathing became very shallow and my heart began racing.

A friend I'd come with held my hand and reminded me to take long, deep breaths but that seemed next to impossible as I got panicky at these sudden and unexpected symptoms. I began to drool uncontrollably and as I tried to raise my right hand to scratch my head I wasn't able to as I seemed to have no strength and little or no control of my motor movement.

This was now truly frightening. I was totally out of control as my body and mind jerked like a marionette before the dictates of the Daime. In that moment I remembered what Paul had told me before the "work" began: "Don't worry, whatever you might experience, you aren't going to die or anything like that." The sensations I now felt seemed to refute that claim. I could only watch and pray it wasn't the real thing.

Small, trivial things were now getting on my nerves. I implored Paul to turn off the music playing in a corner of the room. I was becoming edgy from focusing on things up close. I tried to gaze out the kitchen window to gain some depth to my field of sight in order to try and calm my disorientation. I fought for control over what was happening to me, trying if nothing else to outlast these bizarre feelings. Afterwards I'd reflect on what ensued and consider the term "bad trip" in mulling over my reaction to the Daime.

Paul sat in front of me and a bit off to my right. As I gazed at him imploringly I could see the Daime had also affected him. He sat in his chair without moving, his glasses reflecting indistinct shapes and shadows in the near light. He sat motionless, slowly looking up at me as if struggling to draw himself away from wherever he'd been. He said, "John, you need to let your ego die in the presence of God."

The conviction in his words caught my attention but by that point I was too weak and too lacking in control to do anything but ride the wild wave on top of which I now found myself. His words registered but were soon lost amid my still mounting fear which accompanied what I was experiencing. Later he would confide in me that I'd gone to hell and back.

Writing this now and having asked myself over and over again what can be learned from this encounter, my mind and heart echo with the realization this was a dramatic teaching about my fears: fear of loss of control, fear of dying and even those fears that remain more ambiguous and undefined. The Daime placed me directly in front of these fears. It challenged me to let go and allow the divine presence to which we're all connected come through. My fears blocked that connection and I became lost in an ocean of struggling in a vain attempt to gain power over that which refused to be mastered.

In this terribly bad dream I fell down a shaft without a bottom, searching for any foothold, any crag to grab onto and halt my downward spiral. I realized I'd had too much of a very powerful hallucinogenic that simply overwhelmed my weakened system. In the last analysis the experience showed me the importance of letting go of fear. The Daime, acting in perfect concert with my higher self demonstrated exactly what I still needed to work on.

I was so accustomed to operating from a focus of pain and fear that, true to form, these products of spiritual disconnection continued presenting themselves to me over and over again so I might finally learn the lessons they offered and move forward. They were the reflection of absolute truth shining out at me, blinding me with their pervasive radiance, waiting for the time when I'd finally be able to open, as e.e. cummings said, "the eyes of my eyes," and truly *see* the gifts they offered. In drawing their energies to me I created a bond with them, gave them sustenance and life and, unknowingly, invited their presence into my reality in continually more forceful ways with each new day.

My experience in the Santo Daime work was a powerful reminder of two unresolved facets in my process of becoming whole: I hadn't fully surrendered my ego to God, and attached to that ego were innumerable points of fear trailing behind it like streamers blowing in the wind. In truth my ego was entirely propelled by fear, as that's all I'd ever known. My entire being was protectively encased in an anxiety that continually hemorrhaged more and more of itself. To this point, my surrender had only been partial. While my intention originated in the heartfelt desire to relinquish my ego identity to that which guides us all, the ayahuasca ushered me to the recognition that I still had a tremendous amount of inner work to accomplish before I'd be clear enough to once again pass through those entheogenic portals with the discipline this transformative work demanded.

Even as my journey had become a *process*, so did the continuing lessons, arriving on the coattails of dis-ease, take time to sink into the core of my being before I began to experience mini-epiphanies and connect the self-curative dots. It took ten years of exposing myself to the spiritual energies of the Casa before I came out of my intense, self-generated stupor. When at last I woke up to the big picture, to the fuller, grander story of why it *really* was I'd "discovered" (read: been led to) the transcendent spiritual phenomena responsible for my awakening, I was finally ready to do what needed to be done.

Looking back, I see just how obstinate a case I was, acting out of all my false, stubbornly embraced, self-delusional fantasies. It was vitally important I find forgiveness for myself for having harbored these falsehoods if I was to fully heal. This meant learning to accept and love myself and to cherish the odyssey of enlightenment, which had carried me to this showdown with my inner truth. The following took place early on in my journey into illness at a point where I didn't yet know I was a medium.

Journal entry:

I'm in the process of assimilating the results of a energy-healing session which I had this morning. "Doris" (a pseudonym to protect her privacy) is a woman who's been healing since she was nineteen.

I lay on my bed as she sat in a chair at the foot of the bed and held my big toes between the forefinger and thumb on each of her hands. She recited a request that I be blessed with information and guidance from my Spirit guides and angels and then began to rattle off a series of comments intended for me from my guides and benevolent entities who immediately began channeling through her. Among their comments were the following:

"You need to put away your feelings of shame as you have no reason to feel this way. You are not being punished with this illness and you would help the process of your healing by relaxing and learning to enjoy this time in your life.

You should dispense with the feelings you have that you need to somehow please your helper [my then caregiver] as nothing could be further from the truth of your relationship. You are here together because you are karmically attached to each other and by virtue of this attachment already fulfilling your needs in and through this relationship. He cannot conceive of what you are experiencing and

— 175 —

doesn't fathom the extent to which you and your journey are providing him with a monumentally significant life lesson.

You possess a very strong spirit. Your heart is full of love and your soul is already healed. Now your body is slowly beginning to catch up. You must be patient. You need to extend yourself to others...to make the effort to come out of your exile and to know that others, especially in Abadiania and at the Casa, are waiting to heap their love upon you. They accept you for who you are and couldn't care less about your infirmities."

Wow! If there were ever a further mandate for me to do work I so desperately need to do, this is it. This incident has shaken me out of my complacency and reinforced my need to do a lot more inner work.

My learning curve moved ahead on a steep incline propelled forward by the generosity of Spirit. I'd familiarized myself with the fragmented self and the splintered personality from studying different perspectives on the subject. I now understood these conditions from an objective standpoint. I'd personally experienced the dynamic emotional purge common to the soul retrieval process. One of my Spirit guides had even shown me the circumstances in which I'd endured the same fragmentation in my past, which had led to so many inappropriate behaviors. Melding the prevailing wisdom found in books with a more visceral knowledge gained by passing through adversity formed an experiential milieu rich in both theory and its application.

My refusal to face, accept and embrace many of the aspects of my unwell anima was a profound lesson required by my soul's passage through this life. It also served as a glaring symptom of my paucity of wholeness. Timing continued to be the critical factor in my expanding journey of self-discovery. My loftiest challenges lay not in unearthing broken aspects of my identity, for I was continually uncovering new evidence of their existence. The difficulty lay in overcoming the formidable momentum generated by my old way of viewing self.

Without a convincing, workable plan aimed at altering the way I saw myself, my best intentions, no matter how fervent, ended up hollow and unfulfilled as I quickly resumed old patterns. The burgeoning wisdom I'd slowly acquired about this thing called *consciousness* in addition to having constructed what I thought was a viable strategy to implement newly acquired knowledge weren't potent enough forces to allow me to throw off the yoke of my old ways.

I gradually acquired the perspective and discipline to reconcile the conflicted aspects of my character. Locating my realness within meant entering into a relationship with the indwelling God...a connection I'd come to realize was pivotal in my healing. Without maintaining a strong conviction that I *could* be healed, that I *was* being healed by the direct intercession of Source manifesting through benevolent spirit Entities *and through my own intentions and efforts,* I would never have discovered *how* to fully regain integrity.

• • •

I ARRIVED AT a point where I wanted to enter into a bold, new accord with disease, a shared complicity aimed at replacing my fear and anger at its existence by uncovering why it had come into being in the first place, what its presence could inform me about myself. I understood its biological-genetic component...at least to the degree it was quantifiable within western medicine's paradigm. I'd gleaned its existential significance from my deepening exploration within alternate levels of consciousness. I'd also begun to fathom its energetic signature, the likely lessons it carried and the psycho-spiritual implications of its origin.

I was now after something else, a novel way of interacting with illness meant to provide me fresh insight into how I might continue evolving through its gravitas-laden existence and reach the other side newly whole and intact. I sought ways to develop objective intimacy with it, whereas previously I'd always reeled at the mere idea of its intrusive arrival, frantic to remove myself from its unwelcome proximity, reactive to a point where fear clouded my every thought. I arrived at this decision because fighting it any longer seemed a mistaken gesture, in opposition to discovering and interpreting its true message. Since day one it had been speaking to me. Only now did I finally begin listening. Like so many other aspects in the process of awakening there was a time and a place when I'd be ready to matriculate to the next level of my spiritual education.

In the beginning the presence of illness seemed cipher-like, enigmatic, the turmoil surrounding its existence an attention-sapping digression. In my formidable unconsciousness I'd convinced myself the purpose for its arrival on the scene was punitive. When my fog finally lifted I came to understand that instead of permitting it to determine my outcome, I could focus on the reasons it had manifested and dissect the lessons it offered. I felt I could silence the shrill noise churned up by fear, which always accompanies un-wellness and obscures its far more profound function. By acknowledging its role in bringing me to the realization my view of life had been deeply flawed, incomplete and lacking, I felt that, ultimately, it could also lead me back to the power to change everything as yet unhealed inside.

Over the years as my muscles atrophied more and more and as I became weaker and less able to care for myself, a revelation dawned in me, urging I adopt this new relationship to that which had so thoroughly challenged and shaped me. This seemed a plausible remedy. It allowed me to view illness not as my penance or as some vengeful perpetrator of misery, like the sword of Damocles poised to strike, but as the medium of change it was always intended to be. I'd come to regard illness as a vehicle of transmutation on a psycho-spiritual level. Even as it had entered me I now sought to step inside it to summon its wisdom and garner its teachings.

I was also looking long and hard at death and discovered something amazing. Buoyed by an unending succession of luminous interactions with Spirits, I now possessed a deep faith in the soul's survival beyond the physical body's demise. Transitioning beyond this life to reconnect with my true nature no longer frightened me. Peering inside at my habitual views and attitudes, what I found was that I feared life more than I feared death! I feared confrontation. I feared controversy. Beyond the perceived safety of the status quo,

I feared the incessant ripples of change, which exemplified, in my dread-benumbed mind, onerous interruptions in the predictable fabric of existence, continual challenges to the myriad expectations I'd constructed out of the fear of fear itself.

And while I'd taken some chances and even discovered success in certain pursuits, the fact of the matter is that a lingering anxiety permeated my every action…a vague yet disquieting undercurrent tingeing each and every sense I employed to greet the world. The template for all this apprehension was deeply imbedded in my earliest behavior. Its topography I knew in intimate, excruciating detail. Although I'd never directly confronted its presence, denying its existence was no longer an option.

This realization shocked me almost as much as my neurologist's original pronouncement that I suffered from a terminal illness. The thought-forms I'd created throughout my life, accreting in layer upon fear-laden layer in my energy field, were the *real* source of my unwellness, preventing me from owning enormous personal power and ensuring it would never manifest so long as I continued perpetuating old behaviors. The blockages I'd unwittingly fostered in my energetic body came about because my long cordoned-off emotions, acting as co-conspirators with an unsubduable angst, formed an ideal habitat in which dis-ease could propagate.

At this juncture I was questioning *virtually* everything. Had I created disease and its emotional disequilibrium specifically to *experience* these facets of human existence this time around? And had I tried unsuccessfully in a prior life to address these same issues? Based on my shamanic journey-work along with ongoing communication with my Spirit guides I became convinced this incarnation was a fresh chance affording me the opportunity to complete important unfinished business carried over from past lives.

Why did it matter? With newfound insights illuminating the *why* of my purpose for being in this life I now felt *obligated* to do my promise here the right way this time around. Cognizance of the broad scope of my soul's efforts across recent lifetimes spurred my commitment to fulfilling a sacred duty, the very reason for my existence in the first place. I needed to discipline myself to remain focused on this goal while healing all that still required repair. The entire process often seemed overwhelming. One thing was certain: In order to complete the mission I'd entered this life to carry out, I needed to preserve my body as best I could while my transformation continued to blossom.

• • •

IN LATE 2006, ten years after being diagnosed, I began having marked difficulty swallowing food and liquids. A persistent tickle developed at the back of my throat, coinciding with an ominous new interference in my swallow reflex. That motion, while not impossible, was at least tricky enough to call my attention to the need for heightened vigilance where ingesting any quantity of food was concerned. It was worrisome being even partially deprived of this function, yet it wasn't so pronounced that I felt compelled to return to seeing a neurologist whom I'd last consulted with some three years before.

If I returned to conventional medicine, I knew I'd be met by a fixed interpretation of the disease lodged inside, subjected to a flurry of tests to measure my breathing capacity, swallowing ability and how the symptoms had progressed since my last visit. While I understood the need for such quantification, I knew I'd also be met by quizzical looks from neurologists trying to fathom how I'd achieved continuance into my then tenth "season" against an adversary as unforgiving as A.L.S....all the while having escaped their knowing counsel for so many critical years.

I was confronted with two choices: return to the prevailing medical paradigm I'd said goodbye to and endure the same limiting approach to treatment I'd experienced previously or rely on faith and my imminent return to the Casa for continuing assistance from my discarnate physician. There was no decision to make.

By this time I'd gotten increasingly tired of my body continually reminding me of frailty, challenge and weakness...the collective markers of dominance that illness exerted over me daily. At the same time I reminded myself that although I didn't understand the process in any tangible, readily identifiable way, I *knew* in my marrow that the spirit Entities of the Casa de Dom Inacio were in fact curing me.

I decided to wait until I returned to the Casa to see what treatment "they" advised, knowing beforehand that even after being cared for by them I'd likely have no better indication of what they'd done nor what to expect from their future ministrations. The prevailing sense of gratitude I held in my heart for them quickly dispersed any need to know the precise nature of their treatments as I renewed myself in the faith that had carried me this far.

When I arrived back at the Casa for what then marked my tenth trip to that hallowed site, I was anxious to have my swallowing mechanism restored to normal functioning. Even while continuing to replay the I-am-being-cured tape in my mind and heart, I was unable to exorcise the reality of this forboding new symptom. But it never occurred to me to doubt that I'd receive alleviation from this latest ominous wrinkle in my health. I went before Joao-incorporating-the-Entity, having consciously surrendered my incessant need-to-know in favor of simply accepting whatever might be provided to me. Over the many years of my repeated sojourns to the Casa I'd personally witnessed a plenitude of miraculous healings, slowly arriving at a place of absolute trust in my mind and heart for the power that the site and its discarnate gatekeepers held to transmute sickness of all kinds.

I knew transcending my ego's constant need for control meant I'd feel vulnerable when I least wanted to, yet that was necessary if I was to let go and let God. My ego's arrogance masked a fear of losing its dominion over every aspect of my existence. My blossoming awareness of why I'd chosen to endure this life translated into increasing compassion and empathy for myself. I labored to retool my thinking to accommodate the urgent need to open my heart to deeper levels of acceptance. For someone as guarded in heart as I'd been, this was an uphill battle, one where constant diligence had to take on a mantra-like repetitiveness in order to shift deeply ingrained patterning. I chuckled to myself on realizing that my tendency towards obsessive-compulsive behavior might actually serve a remedial purpose after all.

As I suspected, the Entity told me to sit in the *current*, the special energy "field" that's the mainstay of so much of the healing work at the Casa. I recalled how I'd been swept up in the nervous clamor for immediate gratification and quantifiable results common to newcomers. Excitement at the thought of receiving surgery, whether invisible or visible, was always elevated to near manic levels. The prevailing thinking seemed to be, "If I'm having surgery that must mean I'm being healed." And while certainly true, something as passive as sitting in the current in meditation seemed to imply a less dynamic, less ameliorative recourse to mending ailments. I held similar prejudices and passions when I'd first come on the scene more than a decade earlier.

Yet after numerous consultations with the Entity, having taken note of the ways I'd responded to various Spirit mandated protocols...all on top of having become a keen observer of the different treatments common to the Casa...over time I came away with a new-found respect for the healing power of simply sitting in the current while the extraordinary energy washed over me, permeating every cell in my being. For someone as left brain as I was, this strange new way of *knowing* the benefit of meditating in this extraordinary energy field had the effect of reinforcing my faith in the greater wisdom at work. And while surrender seemed counter-intuitive to the ways in which I'd always asserted myself, over time I came to the realization that aside from free will choices I controlled precious little in life.

After sitting in the current for several weeks I was told one morning I'd receive a surgery in the operating room the following day. As I'd had on average one surgery per visit in previous trips to the Casa, I knew beforehand what to expect. There were about twenty of us destined for individual operations that following bright, sunny morning...all confined to wheelchairs or limping along on crutches or canes...a wave of mobility-challenged humanity eager to cast away our assistive conveyances.

We filed into the surgery room, and those not confined to wheel-chairs took seats as directed by the room attendants. As we sat in silence one of the mediums in charge of the room for that session explained the simple rules we were asked to follow after receiving spiritual surgery and while taking the special herbs: we shouldn't eat pork, drink alcohol or engage in sexual relations until forty days had passed after our individual procedures. Adhering to these basic rules ensured that our natural energies, augmented by further time spent in the current as well as continuing Entity orchestrated adjustments to our energy fields, could be fully utilized in recuperation and healing. We were also warned to be especially cautious immediately post-spiritual operation as our bodies required adequate time to recover from what was no less powerful a procedure than the kind one would receive in a hospital operating room.

Having felt the after-effects of these surgeries many times pre-viously, I knew to expect substantial downtime for at least twenty-four to thirty-six hours afterwards, during which time I'd alternate between extremely deep sleep and lengthy catnaps, all incredibly rich in dreams. Even though I'd only experienced an identifiable physical sensation on one occasion during a surgery, the reality was that these typically painless procedures were far more consequential than their earthly counterparts. I felt that given who was conducting them as well as the surgery's highly evolved *energetic* focus that they were done with an all-inclusive thoroughness that incarnate physi-cians couldn't begin to equal.

Picture in your mind's eye innumerable evolved spiritual beings who've dedicated themselves to helping their brother and sister souls here on the earth plane. From their realm of purity and truth they have only to glance at our auras to see the often tortuous path we've charted for ourselves. They see with utter clarity the myriad illusions cast up by this three-dimensional spiritual school we call Earth. Not only do they understand the *real* root cause of our ailment along with the precise cure for the imbalance but even more crucially know *precisely what it is our sacred souls most greatly benefit from at this exact point in our journey.*

After the medium finished her cautionary explanation regarding our imminent surgeries, we sat quietly huddled together shoulder-to-shoulder in the steadily warming room. With eyes closed and right hands covering the spot on our bodies where the infirmity was located we waited in complete silence. My hand covered my heart because I wasn't able to place it on top of my head, where the problem had originated, without undue exertion. We sat as a group together like this for about twenty minutes, each of us imploring the God we knew and its healing emissaries, the untold spirit Entities of the Casa, to please heal our infirmities. Suddenly Joao-incorporating-the-Entity entered the room and could be heard saying in his deep, resonant voice "In the name of God, these sons and daughters have received their operations."

Several moments later, after the Entity left the surgery room we were advised we could open our eyes and begin filing out of the space. I knew this was my cue to have my caregiver push me in my wheelchair back home where I planned on making a beeline for bed in anticipation of what I knew to be imminent post-op lassitude. I hadn't even gotten to the front entry gates of the Casa de Dom Inacio when I began drooping in my chair and started feeling tremendously tired, as a heaviness took almost complete possession of my senses and body.

When I arrived home my helper assisted me into bed where I took in my surroundings with a final groggy glance. Seeing the mid-morning sun streaming through the open window was my last conscious observation before a profound torpor forced my eyes closed. It was then just after 10 a.m. I awoke next at 6 p.m., decided I was famished, was helped out of bed, ate something and promptly returned to bed and again into a deep slumber. Fourteen hours later, I opened my eyes to bright sun filtering through the shut window and to songbirds announcing their presence in the new day. I'd just slept twenty-one out of the previous twenty-four hours. Over the next two days I would add yet greater blocks of down time before recovering what was for me a semblance of normal energy.

It was a full week later when I first noticed my swallowing was back to normal. I was eating a bowl of acai "pudding" as it's called, a thick pulpy concoction made from the berries of a plant indigenous to the Amazon river area. The purplish mass is sweet, sticky and thick: perfect fodder with which to test one's swallow reflex...not to mention any lingering phlegmatic condition. In mid-bite it dawned on me that I wasn't experiencing *any* difficulty whatsoever in swallowing the concentrated viscous mass. I was instantly overwhelmed with profound gratitude and my tear ducts opened wide as I offered silent prayers to God and His Entities of light.

If this didn't demonstrate my cure-in-progress I was truly blind to the evolution of my miracle's existence. I reminded myself that those suffering from A.L.S. *never* experience improvement in their condition; the disease is marked by progressive, relentless disintegration. If you're lucky the progression will be gradual or even plateau temporarily. Then approaching the start of my eleventh year living with the disease *I'd witnessed verifiable improvement so profound as to leave no doubt what the Entity had told me years prior was indeed coming to pass.*

• • •

THE ROAD THAT delivered me to this point in my journey had proven rocky yet deeply illuminating. For each step I managed to take in the direction of spiritual recuperation, I seemed to take three steps back. Once again the opposing forces of progress and regress were combining to offer an education in the dynamic tension that's an intrinsic part of life. My responsibility was to locate a point of equilibrium between these polarities by accepting that the presence of one didn't negate the other but in fact served to better define it. Life wasn't good or bad, right or wrong, this or that...as I'd believed from an early age. I was beginning to understand that one measure of a healthy existence was being able to weigh seemingly disparate elements to create unity out of apparent chaos, an obligation that came with the new territory of conscious awareness. Reconciliation with the genuine in your core spontaneously generates in an atmosphere where such harmony kindles. One of my crucial tasks was to replace living from expectation with just this kind of even acceptance of actuality.

Bolstered by my father's confirmation of my own long-held suspicions I concluded man's so-called original *sin* is neither a predetermined condition of entry into life nor a continuous facet of existence but just another apocryphal tale we're told to accept as truth. We're easily seduced by illusions that appear substantive because *we've* constructed them from *our own thoughts and feelings* grounded in the categorical embrace of a "reality" we've always *presumed* to be true and complete.

By harboring such beliefs we veer away from the expansiveness of *real* truth. Through blind acceptance of the signs we follow within this wholesale consensus interpretation we unwittingly give tacit approval to the prevailing paradigm to tell us what we should think and feel. Failing to question its legitimacy only acts to reassert its inviolable nature as *the* sole "reality." Through our presumptive acceptance of a plausible dream steadfastly held sacrosanct by the majority and based on tenets populating that oneiric state, we conjure into being most of the existence we see and live.

Reinforced across the span of a lifetime we assume reactive relationships with virtually every facet of our existence until one day, if we're lucky, we wake up from our collective reverie to discover we've only been occupying a series of illusions, a house of mirrors. These false impressions are in fact a brick and mortar dream, a tangible woolgathering where seduced by a relentless socialization process we're likely to never fully awaken from our illusory slumber.

We often catch glimpses of illumination yet opt to resume the safely predictable. A terminal diagnosis throws a wrench into the fluid operation of our life-works. It represents an unyielding mandate for change. It compels us to treat everyday illusions churned up by the collective consciousness in a new, heightened way if we are to survive its conspiracy of separation on any level.

Detaching myself from the dictates of consensus consciousness was a journey I did not enter into easily. I'd been forcibly removed from all my comfort zones, plunged into an abyss of futility and fear where the only known was the sheer weight and force of the unknown. When I finally managed to surface, catch my breath and look around, I discovered a fresh perspective from which to analyze the forces that I'd always allowed to shape my existence.

The convergence of silence and aloneness I'd chosen brought new clarity to my thoughts and, for the first time, earnest comprehension to the work of observing my emotions, the ways in which I'd always reacted to that vast legerdemain commonly known as *life*. It also invested me with a sizeable curiosity into the nature of my being. I was intent on molding meaning out of the groundswell of chaos battering me from all sides.

My questing self sought ways to ascribe significance to trials rooted in separation and pain out of which some defining recapitulation might ensue directing me to deeper lucidity. I asked myself, "What does the life I've both chosen and been given *really* mean?" While by no means a simple question to answer, I found that examining the nature and purpose of my existence was as important to me now as the transformative awakening newly seeded in my heart. And while a ready answer seemed as distant as a far-off galaxy, addressing the issue implied meaning could be found within the process of my search.

Through this sanctified isolation populating an endless succession of days, endowing me with a patience and insight I'd never known before in a triumph of will over situation, I was at last reintroduced to my real self. The significance of that re-introduction… that *remembering* of my essence…cannot be overstated. The very silence encircling me had taught me how to be fulfilled from within. I felt the breath of Spirit accompanying my every move. And while my mind was chock full of questions and new ways of assessing an *actuality* comprising multiple layers of consciousness, my body longed for further signs of improvement like miraculously having my swallowing restored.

Like an echo, I continually hear in my mind the response the Entity offered to the question I'd posed to him: "When will I begin to see physical improvement?" He'd replied, "There isn't a specific day in which it will be done," *it* meaning my return to wholeness. If it wasn't destined to happen by a certain day or time, then what did his answer mean? As a veteran of many Casa visits and numerous interactions with the Entities, I'd grown accustomed to replies to my queries that were often phrased in a manner that made me re-think both my question and the Entity's response from a much broader context.

I'd learned the Entity's replies often served a didactic, spiritual obligation to one's continued growth first and foremost. Addressing the questioner's desire for a definitive answer that assuaged a left-brain need for empirical evidence didn't always happen. Over time I came to understand what *hadn't* been said was as important as what had been stated. Fathoming this subtle distinction enabled deeper trust in the intuitive wisdom of my higher self and created a meaningful antidote to solely looking externally for answers.

The Entity's careful choice of words also spoke to the nature of my journey in such a way as to suggest an *evolving process.* It contained ingredients of growth, change and healing, yet focused on that processes's existence as a sustained phenomenon absent a beginning, a middle or an end. Put a different way, there was an actual *beingness* to the journey I'd embarked on in lieu of its acting solely as a conveyance to funnel me to an ultimate end result. The implication was that learning would inevitably happen while I was passing through the entire process. From the standpoint of the timelessness defining the soul's evolution, it makes perfect sense. What remained was the importance of embracing the journey itself and not being overly concerned with the outcome. This in turn demanded even deeper levels of patience as one of my primary soul lessons.

Over time and with the Entity's repeated admonishments that I *was*, in fact, healing, I learned to release my death grip in focusing only on physical survival, instead channeling my formidable energies into cultivating an environment that more fully supported my evolving awakening. This included praying for greater insight into my spiritual mission as well as finding significant ways in which to shepherd others along their own paths toward truth and wholeness.

As mute and physically challenged as I'd become, this often meant simply offering others the reassurance of my smile in the absence of dialogue, yet it was enough. All the hours I'd spent in disillusionment, despair and the deprivation of companionship now coalesced.

Journal entry:

Here's what I'm beginning to understand for the very first time: my expectations have been nothing more than attempts at controlling my universe. Control is, for me, a very important and pivotal word. When I say "controlling my universe," it's meant an all-or-nothing kind of scenario. Either things required by way of my "expectations" met fruition by those from whom I "expected" or, more often, the expectation was so unreasonable from the get-go that any participant's efforts were doomed to failure.

All this existed in my mind in a kind of elaborate daydream, a continuing cry for order in what has been my out-of-control universe. Clearly, this issue can be traced back to my early youth when for reasons becoming less ambiguous, I sought out any control in a world that refused to provide me the nurture I desperately needed.

If someone didn't do precisely what I expected of them they were fair game to be excommunicated from my cabal of confederates. The extraordinarily presumptuous thing about this contrived world was I almost never verbalized these expectations to others. I simply assumed for some inexplicable reason they'd somehow deduce what I demanded of them and kowtow to my wishes.

This has the makings of what crazy people do. And in fact that, in its worst fabrication, was who I'd become...detached, if not from reality, then at least from reasonable, rational thought.

Now as the successive layers of my emotional and psychological selves are being peeled away, the truth of my expectations' control over me, not over others, is revealing itself. This is all awash in irony. In my attempt to exert maximum influence in my world I did little more than create maximum interference with the truth.

My mission now is to ferret out all of the times when I expect something, anything, of others and carefully weigh it against the barometer of dispassionate reason. Searching out my personal truth has become as important to me as drawing breath.

What I discovered was that the pure traits of soul we carry into life from the other side are always accessible, awaiting our free-will decision to seize upon their wisdom. By choosing these as models, we welcome cleansing change into our lives. The nemesis to expansion lies in the potential for its polar opposite to manifest, creating an environment of contraction. By thinking, feeling and intending a life based in qualities of soul grounded in the truth and presence of our *elemental* form we signal our openness to absorb the essence of all they have to offer. They become behavioral elements we enact intentionally into our daily rituals. In this way we're able to continually draw higher spiritual energies to ourselves to reinforce the healing dynamic we've set into motion through free will.

I learned that it's precisely how we prize ourselves as individual souls in these vessels of flesh that we're able to create an atmosphere of veneration for others. From the place of wholeness, which is love of self, springs compassion and the means through which to honor our fellow souls. Absent the presence of love, we operate from deficit, incapable of offering to others that which we ourselves do not possess. We model wholeness or incompleteness to ourselves by what we choose to think and feel, mirroring these choices to others from cues we select from our truest, most profoundly real selves, our souls.

Our judgmental interpretations of a limited sensory "reality," which surrounds and often besieges us, fosters disconnection through lack of discipline. If our way of engaging "reality" isn't regulated by scrutinizing and sifting out fallacy, we run the risk of reveling in a fool's paradise, lulled into self-deception. The easy path is apparent. It's the one I'd always chosen, mesmerized by the ignis fatuus of my epic emotional disenfranchisement. The choice between blind acceptance and self-disciplined attentiveness is the difference between free will and obedience. As my father offered from his newly found perch on the other side: *"There's two ways to live life: lost below the current or on the banks of the river watching it. Learn to watch yourselves."*

What this realization signified to me was that, at a very young age, I'd quite literally made the most soulgrowth-appropriate choice about how to be in this world. That "error" in direction served a brilliant purpose, funneling me to experience the precise elements required for my soul's evolution in this incarnation. That meant learning how to open my heart, ushered to the need through dis-ease. My first opening to my real heart-self...to my core truth...came eight years prior to my diagnosis through the medium of art.

• • •

GIVING MYSELF INCREASING permission to expand beyond the self-limiting boundaries I'd set early on, the world I knew slowly tilted on its axis in the direction of a fervent awakening. While still oblivious to the true depth of its significance I sensed the importance of honoring my muse, my inner voice. This first began for me at the age of thirty-seven when I finally approved of the artist I'd always been and started creating in earnest. Prior to that determined plunge into mixed media sculpture, I'd only briefly listened to my creative urges, even though my imaginative nub incessantly prodded me with inspiration and the powerful urge to *make stuff*.

From the very beginning neither my parents nor family were able to comprehend my deep-seated passion to create. That led to repeated confrontations between us at a crucial time in the early development of my creative sensibility. Believing I was only a child at play, my parents tended to pay well-meaning lip service to my earnest attempts at invoking my muse. What that *child at play* sought to create in those early years was his very own self through the initiatory rite of art. Being spurned by misunderstanding from those I most sought validation from...added to already sizeable feelings of emotional abandonment...the way in which my selfhood was defined short-circuited, not to re-emerge until decades later. Stymied by a lack of support, I gave up on *the* essential characteristic expressing who I am.

In my late 30's I finally reconnected with a part of me deeply and intrinsically tied to my spirit and to the passion of who I really was. In creating art I felt joined with an energy of purity and emotion I often experienced in an vibratory way as a new, enlivening energy flowing through me. Time receded from my conscious awareness. I began to consider what I was *feeling* for the very first time. Although a far cry from any deep, insightful gaze inward, it was through these initial, tentative glimpses at parts of me long suppressed where the faint stirrings of change were first implemented. In place of any longer denying the dream I'd held, like so many other parts of me, in abeyance for decades, I was determined to create. Creating art became a metaphor for creating my long missing true self.

Lo and behold, what I began to observe in my creations were thinly disguised messages from my subconscious mind and from my long sequestered heart telling me just how profound the pain was that I'd kept bottled up inside. Looking back at the art I made then, I see consistent references to my inner turmoil, even though I couldn't have verbalized these emotions at that time. Through the insightful but occult vocabulary of artistic expression, I was initiated into discovering the truth.

The heart. My heart. Initially I had a difficult time processing my newly discovered emotions. I'd been living in a world so emotionally closed off, so out of alignment with the bona fide energies of my soul, that when I first started to feel what I'd never felt before, I was often on edge, rubbed raw by all I was experiencing. It took a very long time to allow these newly unbridled sentiments to simply *be* before I was able to look in the mirror and nod knowingly at the lightness of being I now felt.

From the advent of my first symptoms I'd begun keeping a detailed journal of my day-to-day experiences, insights, reflections, and moods. I'd journaled before and always felt the purge of words to be a creative, insightful form of self-expression. In my post-diagnosis writing I'd thrown a few pity parties but soon discovered the only one consistently in attendance was myself. Tiring of that unproductive pursuit I took to recording the details of my, thankfully, few dark moods as well as the elation I experienced each time my Spirit helpers saw fit to christen me with some new baptism of insight. All of this served its intended catharsis and provided the detailed record for this book.

Just as art opened me up to my true feelings so too did the process of journaling serve in the rediscovery of self and heart. It might be said that I slowly wrote and created my way back to health. In the process of writing down my thoughts and the jumble of emotions enabling them, I began to see patterns of behavior. Through creative self-discernment, it was only a matter of time until I was able to unravel and separate the strands of truth emerging from my long guarded false reality. The long cordoned-off reaches of my heart grew more accessible as I continued dissecting old behaviors and gradually cleansed my emotional core.

My desire to change my life overcame my long-held reluctance to change. I was ushered along the winding route I'd created for my soul's lessons by Spirit guides exercising infinite patience and love without qualification. I was asked to dig deep in order to locate the strength this continuing odyssey demanded of me. And though I squandered inordinate chunks of precious time in continued homage to the various gods of my invented consciousness, I finally began to come around. I now realize I was shown the way to wholeness so my odyssey might serve to inspire others to be unafraid to initiate their own healing path. In this there is a beautiful purpose and a much grander design than simply that of my own return to wholeness.

Journal entry:

I welcomed a gifted light worker into my home yesterday. She's an energy worker and intuitive who reads people's energy fields, channels angelic presence,' orchestrates spiritual "clearings" and peers into past lives.

One clear message from Spirit: I only have to ask for help and it will come to me. Dad, my deceased brother, David, the archangel

Michael, and a powerful protector guardian known as Samuel were all in attendance. Their message was clear: I've taken this body, this life and this disease to learn patience, to learn empathy and to provide a beacon of light to others.

The session clarified some aspects of previous readings and channelings while elaborating on the message that, ironically, even with my disabilities, if not precisely because of them, I'm here to help others heal.

This feels very true to me. I know its resonance in my heart to be validation of my most profound spiritual purpose. She exclaimed my auric energy was dramatically more pronounced in area than normal which she attributed to my innate strength and ability to heal.

What helped me most in this session was receiving the reminder that all the enormous frustration, pain and aloneness I've experienced these many years serves a didactic purpose in allowing me to better empathize with the disconnection from truth and love so many others suffer from. Having been there myself, I hold no small amount of compassion for my fellow man.

10

An Examined Life

WHEN I WAS a sophomore in high school taught by the Christian Brothers of Ireland in the no-holds-barred manner of discipline still in vogue at the time, one of my teachers expounded enthusiastically one day on the French mystic and philosopher Pierre Teilhard de Chardin. This introduction to philosophy was fascinating. After school let out I walked down to a used bookstore and bought two of the author's books. A short time afterwards, the teacher who'd raved about de Chardin's impressive intellect spied the books tucked under my arm. He stopped me in the hallway and asked, "So, do you understand de Chardin?" In no way able to fathom de Chardin's words, yet eager to respond, I meekly replied, "Yes, but so far only the conjunctions."

Like my earnest attempts at understanding de Chardin I was now, years later, at long last trying to locate and understand my real self, moving out of the cycle of fear and doubt that had plagued me from my earliest recollections. In this new space my true self had a safe harbor from which to expand into fullness. While I came to the search for a physical cure feeling bereft of any personal power, it was precisely within the sensation of powerlessness where I first discovered the seed of my genuine strength. That strength was discovered in the act of uncovering my authenticity.

I came to understand that uncovering my core genuineness and validating myself could only come after I'd hit rock bottom, and my newfound awareness...my expanding perceptual cognizance...had time to assimilate the many new potentialities pointing me towards a fresh beginning. As I created balance out of disequilibrium, my sizeable antipathy slowly gave way to a fresh heart-centered embrace of life.

The tentative budding of a newly empowered self sprang miraculously from a place deep within, supporting the feeling I'd come full circle. I arrived at the doorstep of truth after a protracted journey through the wasteland of emotional addiction. The discovery of true internal power, appearing like a phoenix rising from the ashes of my historical disempowerment, renewed my faith in the limitless good flowing from Source...a wellspring I discovered was as immanent as it was external.

By gradually recalling the presence of love suffused within my soul I reconnected with what I'd given up on so long ago: my heart and its formidable truths. Though I didn't consciously equate recollection of true self with the concept of remembering my true source in fact that's precisely what it was. While my heart was blocked off from the candor of feeling I experienced an almost total disconnection from that remembrance, the memory of my inherent perfection as a creation of the divine.

What revealed itself to me in my protracted return to wholeness was a fundamental truth: there is no separation between our world of phenomena and the realm of Spirit. We just think there is. Like the personal stupor I'd created and so fearfully occupied, accepted reality is often just a series of contrived illusions whose messages mesmerize us into grasping after material objects to gain a sense of control that is otherwise lacking. Illusion's counterpoint is the realm of Spirit: a domain of pure essence devoid of constant judgments, which are the albatross of man's birthright.

It is a self-fulfilling prophecy that I became the story I told myself. Almost from the beginning, my dialogue with self and with the world was skewed, lopsided, madly tilting toward the dictates of an emotional paucity I felt like some blunt prod continually poking me in the ribs. Its language became my dialect of pain, binding up my heart in innumerable strands of fear, lack and isolation. In reciting this story over and over again in my mind, heart and throughout my being...colored as it was by those beliefs and fears I staunchly adhered to...I sanctioned disconnection from my authentic self instead giving permission to my assumed persona to call the shots.

When the spigot containing my emotional nurture ceased flowing, everything in my world changed. Whether the current truly stopped or I somehow mistakenly sensed it ended is immaterial: the consciousness I labored under screamed with finality, "It's gone!" In large part my story had been one of lack, a narrative of loss of power and authenticity, and how ultimately I was able to regain them. These defining facets of my personal story lie at the basis of my return to wholeness.

Power takes many forms, some beneficial, some detrimental. In society power is often seen and valued for its external quality, a glossy surface manifestation revered for its illusion of strength. Actual power is distinguishable by its capacity to blend resolve with empathy, to combine afflatus with the quest to know self, in order to commit more fully to the exercise of compassionate ideals. It's entirely internal, with no need of the gaudiness by which its external other is best known. For actual personal power to be present, the comfort of fear must be eschewed for the light of truth.

At the core of the mind-body-spirit synthesis lies this point: If we choose to invalidate the pain that informs us with its instructive message, we automatically empower it. Arriving at a place where genuine power can form and mature involves fostering conscious intention and upholding the obligation to venerate truth. This requires dismantling the hollow shadows of fear that attempt to coax us away from our sacred selves. Authentic power is achievable when taking responsibility for the way you walk in the world supersedes the spellbinding illusion of everyday waking reality, and you consciously choose to step out of the dream. Chief among my lessons was learning to discriminate my contrived reality from the *actuality* modeled by love.

Once I'd changed the frequency of my thinking and feeling I began attracting congruous vibrations into my life and changes in my thought-feeling field occurred at a vastly accelerated rate. As I've said, one of the key components in that frequency shift was *gratitude.* If someone had told me early on in my odyssey I'd arrive at a point where gratitude would replace the constant seeking after answers, solutions and cures, I would've questioned how they could've come to such an implausible conclusion. Transmuting my thoughts and feelings was the threshold experience that brought all my other efforts into alignment with the wholeness I sought. Gratitude was the natural extension of that awakening into consciousness.

The leap of faith required to find gratitude in the midst of pain often signifies surrender to a higher power and adoption of a greater purpose. Just as one moves through Kubler-Ross's classic transitional stages in any crisis, similarly the discovery of grace inside pain's swirling storm is evidence of further self-actualization in the process of healing. Each of us is born into this life with the energy of a greater purpose pulsating from the inner recesses of our soul. It's our responsibility to bring that whispering desire into concrete form in the world and obey its bliss-filled imperative. In choosing to die to the world's ensorcelling fictions we create space in which to regenerate into wholeness. We overcome illusion to find rebirth in the truth our hearts unceasingly chant to us. We possess enormous power, nothing less than the power to resurrect ourselves.

In the process of invoking more ways in which to express gratitude for the abundance I could now finally see, was how it simultaneously brought more lightness and joy into my being while acting as a reminder that my connection to the perfection of Source made me already perfect. I didn't have to be some idealized notion of a person. I didn't have to conform to standards others set. I'd tried all that and it had never worked, never felt right. Instead, by diligently paying attention to the cues self-examination provided me concerning healthy change, I discovered my real self.

During this crucial time I often thought to myself, Where has all the anger, rage and frustration gone I used to feel? While by no means entirely free of these old traveling companions, as I gained increasing clarity on how to author my new beginning, my spiritual re-purposing, these facets of fear exerted less and less of a gravitational pull on the energy field of my emotions. Just as I'd challenged society's expectations regarding my prognosis I was now examining the very *qualities* of mind and heart forming the *who* that had been masquerading as *me* with such chameleon-like subterfuge for so long.

Without being consciously aware of it, I'd spent my entire life trying to get back in touch with the bereaved child residing within my depths. My endeavors were always incomplete, unfulfilled, destined to reside in my deepest longing as a condition of an unquenchable desire for emotional closure. Incapable of being persuaded into the present moment, that child adamantly remained behind, locked up deep inside, abhorring the abandonment it still felt without surcease, yet refusing to leave the safety of its prison. Likewise, an integral and pivotal part of me remained unavailable in the present moment, creating intense discord in my emotional balance. It reminded me of a line in one of Rilke's poems: "...in you, who were a child once—in you."

Right living requires successful stewardship of the heart. All life ever taught me about my emotional center was contained in the unspoken grief I carried in that constricted space. The scales of happiness and sorrow always felt perilously tipped toward the sad side. Not being a good custodian responsible to his honest feelings, the one thing I did trust in was that the sorrow, anger and loneliness bottled up inside could never see the light of day. I clamped down tight on the vessel holding in these feelings, angst-ridden about ever giving voice to the torment I felt.

I didn't struggle with the truth for the truth had become so obscured by my efforts to impose my will on an unacceptable world it had long since ceased being clear to me. It was a commodity no longer imbued with meaning in my life, permanently invalidated by my epic separation from anything poised to cause me further torment. Ignorant about why I was battling in the first place didn't lessen the intensity of, nor the number of campaigns I waged against, my nemesis. The primary ingredients in the daily porridge I fed myself were denial and a reactive unconsciousness. They nurtured the false assurance which arises when the self assumes a defensive posture. They were the scar tissue concealing my deepest pain. They alone guaranteed if not a perfect world then at least one with marginally palatable terms of my own choosing.

I'd become a self-enabling dweller in illusion: obsessively attending to the myriad fictions of my compulsively acted-out charade as if dressed for a costume party, donning any disguise if it meant I didn't have to view myself unmasked or be seen by others with my flaws laid bare. I came to view vulnerability as an aberrant biological condition, a clever little ruse nature employed to lure me into letting down my guard. But I was too smart for that ploy. I'd learned early on that all openness and emotional honesty had ever gotten me was a deeply bruised psyche and a lacerated heart. The single most important thing I could do was to never allow this to happen again.

From a very early age my life got off on the wrong track as the momentum of my contrived reality built up more and more steam. In the process of living in this hermitage of grossly inappropriate and continually unrequited expectations, I slowly but surely widened the gap between myself and rational self-awareness. Detaching from consensus reality, I carried the torch of the superficial, in my disjointed thinking quick to extol the merits of a sham hallucination so complete in its manifest dupery that it assumed a life of its own.

The catalyst responsible for infusing some much needed insight into my emotional vacuum was the same beneficent source I'd first encountered at the Entity's sacred waterfall. After experiencing the waterfall, my body, mind and heart radiated a bliss, a calm and a joy previously unimaginable. At a far deeper, more profound level my soul was introduced to a primal grace, which soothed my spirit's intense longing for purpose while rendering its yearning into a profound new perception flooded with meaning.

Far from being a linear process this awakening realization provided no tangible frames of reference to explain what could, in the end, only be understood at the juncture where faith converged with surrender. In this way my soul sought numinous amplitude and its undeniable birthright into fullness. Through the embrace of this reconnection, my soul rediscovered its natural element even while sense clamored for its counterpoint in flesh and blood, trial and error.

• • •

BEYOND THE HEART-POUNDING shock of its discovery the first response to receiving a terminal diagnosis is, Why me, why now? If our lives are quests for meaning, there exists no more compelling motivation to construct some defining purpose out of our journeys than through the mortal immediacy wreaked by the advent of disease. Such news is an act of intervention between body and Spirit, a call to reconnect what's been severed or allowed to wither, a summons to identify what's lacking, a void that disease has unerringly filled. The child within me required this spiritual mediation in order that the man who still anxiously cradled him inside could move past being stuck and grow his soul.

When I was *led* to the understanding of why I'm here, possessed of this body, submitting to this particular life experience, confronting specific lessons that are elements in this chosen existence, I was able to make sense out of what had always been an incomprehensible blur. For the first time I was able to comprehend the significance and purpose of my life in the context of a much greater design. I was able to visualize my role in the spiritual continuum as simultaneously unique from while still connected to the vast wheel of life. I came to think of this function of the individual spirit as the path of personal ascendency. Illness demonstrated an unfulfilled need while defining a transcendent purpose.

Travail emboldens a mechanism of change deep within. It informs our essence that something is profoundly imbalanced. It shocks us with the recognition it's capable of sundering our spirit and destroying the flesh if we fail to heed its warning. As I probed my character to isolate, explore and clear away aspects of self not aligned with truth, so too was illness probing me to isolate and test those same aspects of discord in a paradoxical dance of inversion. Once my fog of fear lifted I began a new relationship with dis-ease...one which promised a solution to its wrath.

All the while I stubbornly held onto my vision of a cure-in-progress, the notion of which, brimming in my cells, acted as adjuvant therapy, while I grappled with the substance and implication of living in the tutoring moment. I'd reached a place where my views had been drastically altered by all the epiphanies cascading down on me. I was changed and changing at a vastly accelerated rate, the product of conscious intention combined with higher purpose. I considered the wisdom of the Sufi master and poet, Hafiz, who'd said: "...this is the time for you to deeply compute the impossibility that there is anything but grace."

Suffused within the religion of my upbringing was the implicit message that man, by the very nature of his tarnished birthright into original sin, was fragmented, unfulfilled, less than whole. Through reliance on an expectant, often punitive God who precipitated forgiveness through sacerdotal functionaries, one could be washed clean and grace could supplant its contrary foe...at least temporarily. Sin was, after all, recidivistic by definition of the human condition, creating an atmosphere of continuing need only met through repeated pit stops at the confessional. Combined with the requisite supplication one's access to forgiveness was moderated by intermediaries doling out arbitrary penance while vouchsafing pardons with the piety of demigods.

Couched in an ancient tongue and cloaked in mysterious ritual, one's entry into heaven, that fabled berth of ultimate compensation for having chosen appropriate earthly endeavors, was attainable only by those bowing to prescribed doctrine. Spiritual self-reliance was a vague myth, neither discussed nor touted. This attitude of reliance not on self but on intermediaries only exacerbated an already disconnected psyche, breeding distrust in my inner voice and in its place capitulation to external dictates too often tethered to the ulterior motives of others and to agendas in no way harmonious to my spirit. My father's comments from beyond this life provided a refreshing counterpoint of truth to such fables of disconnection.

In the end, while my passage through these times shaped my perspective, I no longer had any interest in pointing an accusing finger at the religious indoctrination which came with my elementary schooling. Neither did I intend to continue railing against its underlying beliefs and exclaim bitterness at its exclusionary practices, for I arrived at the realization that the notion of belief is a personal choice, as is the choice of adopting wholeness and wellness outside doctrinal boundaries.

That history, while a poignant reminder of a bleak, troubling time in life, informed my soul in what disconnection from self, society and Source felt like. That desultory lack paved the way for a much deeper appreciation of love when at last my heart was able to identify its presence. When it became clear I could and should rely on love, I entered into direct relationship with Source (or rather re-established my unbroken bond with my own Godliness). In doing so I saw the falsity and presumptuousness of allowing anyone else to mediate between myself and what I was already a spark of: the Divine.

I was after an understanding of something far deeper than a collection of dogmatic principles, arcane rituals and censer smoke. I sought the *causes* that contributed to my spiritual disenfranchisement, to my life getting off on the wrong track. The religion foisted on me in my youth was only another symptom of unconscious sameness. Like the Palmer method of penmanship espoused by my early teachers, it, too, sought to stifle self-expression in exchange for the mind-numbing ritual of an ordered predictability, which endeavored to define what was deemed "correct" as well as pigeonhole the undefinable.

• • •

WHETHER CONSCIOUS OR not of its existence, man constantly seeks transcendence in his trek across life's revelatory landscape. By its very temporality, he knows his flesh-laden vessel cannot survive time's ravages. In searching for meaning beyond the physical shell and the constraining illusions of this world, he bargains for a slice of the immortal. The quest for permanence outside himself, yet still connected to what resides at his core, is undertaken to perpetuate some trace of his essence beyond his demise. Illness delivered me to a spiritual quest for such transcendence, even as it brought me to an encounter with facets of my persona long obscured and stymied. As I discovered, the reality was that these two journeys were one and the same.

Having worked hard to divest myself of my "Catholic overnighter"...the polarizing baggage of guilt, of right and wrong, of heaven and hell, of good and bad I'd acquired on my parochial junket...I prepared to enter the quest fortified by the expansive narrative of Spirit-led intervention illuminating my route. In a real way, *knowing* I was being healed freed up valuable energies to invest in the task of much deeper self-assessment. I felt I could locate a defining point of consummate association with the same loving bliss I'd connected with at the Entity's sacred waterfall. A brief entry in my journal encapsulates what I was attempting to do as I sought an unclouded channel to Spirit.

Journal entry:

And while the surrendering self expands and grows by emptying itself of control, it's still met with the obstinate and controlling ego, which desires nothing more than to unseat such spiritual altruism from its soapbox.

My search for meaning continued unfolding as a sustained *process*, providing me the insights and intuitive knowings I needed most at the exact point my soul required them. Over a span of more than four decades I'd slowly and methodically created imbalances in my emotional energy field through the unhealthy ways I chose to interpret the world...all of which eventually culminated in dis-ease in my physical organism. Was the predisposing genetic factor already present in my system? Of course. Did it require a trigger to implement its destructive activity? Absolutely. The dynamic of my errant intentions opened a unitive channel between the hibernating gene and my equally errant emotions. My confused intentions served as archetypes for behaviors at cross-purposes with my body's equilibrium, yet in so doing created a vital lesson tailored to match my soul's deepest need.

I could have continued disregarding love and persisted in armoring my heart. I could have chosen to ridicule the notion of spirit Entities and their promises to cure me. I could have decided to give up and die. I could have chosen any path. What I chose was the path of my highest, most perfect lesson and, at the fork in the road, opted in favor of pain instead of grace. While that was the "easy" choice, either decision would've ultimately ushered me to the identical end result. I began this odyssey apoplectic with fear. Love's presence transmuted that fear into an abiding, informed faith, a faith grounded in love.

As admirable as my intentions are to persevere in the work of evolving and healing, I know the nature of my sojourn will continue to challenge me at every turn with the constant need for self-discipline. Along with exerting control over thoughts, emotions and their potent energies comes reaffirmation of the need to maintain vigilant conscious awareness. The resolve and strength I've gained through my new self-actualized choices, will act as continuing markers of how far I've traveled to arrive at this moment. My life will continue being my greatest artistic creation, provided I firmly hold that as my intention and continue dreaming the dream into fruition. It's an ever-expanding work in progress: a fluid, evolving continuum now connected to my higher self in conscious equilibrium.

• • •

THERE REMAINS MUCH work to do. Today, as I begin my eighteenth year since diagnosis, physical symptoms of the illness persist. Both my index fingers are losing strength along with the ability to straighten out. While this loss of function may seem trifling when compared to the truly vital necessities of breathing and swallowing, for someone lacking a voice the inability to point at needed objects signifies one less coping tool at the ready. An emotional tipping point occurs when the realization strikes me that I've become yet *further* compromised physically. This prompts frustration, which, in turn, engenders those old, familiar pangs of resentment at my body not performing correctly. I have a long history of not liking or loving myself, stretching far back even before elementary school. This acquired behavioral matrix is so deeply embedded in my subconscious, loosening its grip often seems an Augean pursuit.

These days I'm dedicated to the work of learning how to more fully love myself, accepting myself not *in spite* of my challenges but precisely *owing* to their presence in my daily world. As my physical body becomes increasingly more impaired by the disease...albeit in a thankfully snail's paced way...I'm asked to provide it greater and greater emotional nurture. If there's a paradox in my journey it is this. How can you love a body whose lack of smooth functioning challenges any longanimity you thought you possessed?

I understand this for what it really is: an ongoing skirmish with parts of my former self inclined to allow anger control over me. After all, anger is simply fear in disguise. Specifically, fear of loss of control masked as frustration. Understanding this and being conscious of it create space in which such illusion-based impediments to the truth of love can be dispersed. I see the choice of heart awareness over fear's constriction as some of my most critical instruction. Constant vigilance is required to anticipate the forceful ways that fear hiding behind frustration colors one's thoughts and feelings, along with discovering new and self-affirming ways to diffuse and transmute its energy into something positive.

As with so many other facets of my journey toward wholeness, the lingering temptation is to give up, give in and allow old habits free rein. I often reflect on why I'm still knee-deep in this battle, still fighting what frequently feels like overwhelming obstacles, still challenged by this game of solitaire I often play with the deck of hours. Having weathered years of adversity, I appreciate from a point deep within the center of my being how profoundly fatiguing such unremitting struggle is. Lasting this many years against an adversary as potent and merciless as this one, I've acquired a survivor's knowing mindset and a begrudging acceptance of certain things.

I alternate between eulogizing what the disease has taken from me and elegizing precious functions that still remain intact. My struggle has more to do with me, past, present and still to come, than with the notion or residence of illness. I remind myself a stubborn will hasn't hurt my survival. And I'm quick to remember that my prayers coupled with a faith informed by trial are facilitating changes subtly, just enough below the surface of my sensory awareness that I can't yet perceive of their blossoming.

In an environment so pregnant with change, the clarity of my new path and purpose often shares a strange bedfellow with what lies in opposition. Pain still occupies the same quarters as grace. Faith coexists alongside doubt. Fear inhabits the hollow and lonely places when courage is nowhere to be found. My journey touches all these things. It's an odyssey both profound and profoundly common. As a good friend often reminded me, "You're not special, John." Her statement was direct and honest: although my struggles and challenges may be daunting and even poignant, there are many, many others sharing equal if not greater difficulties. All I have to do is look around me for ready evidence of not being in the minority.

Misery doesn't always love company. My greatest lessons were learned in pain-filled silence with no one else around. Finally acknowledging the at times ugly truth of who I'd become was a prerequisite to implementing the change I'd avoided like the plague. When I opened my ears, pain and silence both spoke to me. They had much to say about the error of my ways. They asked me to grow past my self-imposed limits, to become the truth I'd brought with me into this life from the the realm of soul. They intervened through illness because my stubbornness was adamant and epic. In the end I listened to them and learned what no one had ever taught me before. Opening my heart was the solution to *all* my ills...even my terminal one.

In gaining the perspective required to step outside my self-absorbed story, compassion for the suffering of others was given an opportunity to at last blossom in what had been my fear-choked heart. Learning to remove myself, at least temporarily from the constant drama dis-ease has us believe about ourselves, created a much needed space in which new, healthier perspectives could be nurtured and the bedrock of my long-held beliefs examined.

While my struggles contain all the facets of formidable difficulty, the insight building in my heart-mind is that my true power lies in how I choose to face these torments. My success or failure *attitudinally* in any given day and, ultimately, in the entire journey of life itself is determined by me and me alone. I'd known this intellectually and philosophically but needed to persuade my emotional center this concept could no longer exist as just another maxim from some self-help seminar. It required my direct intention and attention if it were to become part of my conscious, new life practice and substantively inform the choices I made moving forward.

Many of the decisions I arrived at during my incarceration by illness have excluded others from sharing my journey. I didn't set out to intentionally deny access to my newly challenged life, yet in coming from a place so firmly entrenched in my historical mindset, that's precisely the environment I unwittingly created. Add to this the disconnecting effect my speechlessness had on my interaction with others, as well as any latent fears concerning illness they already harbored, and the disease acting in concert with my choices created a setting in which a kind of social leprosy took shape, excluding me from just the kind of contact with others from which I would've greatly benefited. This is the isolation I learned to befriend in long overdue self-appraisal as I made it an accomplice in my gradual return to wholeness.

• • •

THE TENDENCY I observed in others sharing my grim diagnosis was to grab at almost any "new" modality promising if not an outright cure then at least symptomatic amelioration. While I shared the thinking that doing something constructive in trying to thwart illness's dominion over me was preferable to sitting, as my mother used to say, "like a lump on a log"...in my mind, pursuing what in the vast majority of cases turned out to be empty promises seemed more a game of cat and mouse and less about viable alternatives to dying. Chasing after chimeras wasn't adequate reason for engaging my already taxed energies, simply for the sake of appearing busy.

For us who'd become unintentional kin by virtue of sharing the same affliction, any signs of *plateauing* were as desperately sought after as they were enthusiastically welcomed. Time held a double meaning for each of us: the hopeful blessing for continuance pitted against the all too real curse of impermanence...colliding head-on in a winner-take-all contest. In the early days post-diagnosis I was as frantic as anyone to find a way out of my dilemma. I told myself it was important at the very minimum to *try* and survive...knowing as I did the chances of success seemed to lay somewhere between slim and none. All that changed when the Entity said, "I will cure you." I felt an exhilarating sense of relief, incredulity and gratitude move through me in a vibratory rush.

Journal entry:

Entering the uncharted landscape of disease is like embarking on a vision quest. Utter lack of certainty in knowing what you'll encounter means submitting to all the void might bring.

By stepping into the unknown with the desire to be transformed, at least spiritually, you prepare yourself to suffer the lessons of illness with a patience informed by the fuller purpose of your path. At least that's the concept you try and maintain.

Courage offers one way in which to carry yourself forward into such unfamiliar terrain. In my case that wasn't available. Instead fear acted as my propulsion, impelling me toward what began as a journey through illness yet culminated in the pursuit of my own long absent spiritual integrity.

I made the decision short of the discovery of a cure for A.L.S. I'd simply follow the Entity-mandated protocols and leave the rest to faith, doubly blessed to have discovered both an alternative to my demise along with a clear path to desperately needed inner healing. I often pondered whether I was doing enough by subscribing to this regimen alone, yet this path resonates throughout my being in ways like nothing else does. If I've learned nothing else, it's to follow such messages springing forth from my inner voice. Maintaining faith in my benefactors working from the other side of the veil feels especially important, as if forgetting their pivotal role in my odyssey would be a blasphemy against those primarily responsible for my salvation.

The blessing of having survived far beyond both my original prognosis as well as substantially past the average life expectancy for someone with this disease brings with it the realization that I no longer possess the same fortitude I had when this journey began. I'm often physically, mentally or emotionally fatigued: unwavering components of the intense, prolonged marathon I've been "running." I've had to jettison many of the taken-for-granted conveniences of my previous life, paying homage instead to the gods of necessity, uncertainty and to trusting in all I really can't ever know. I've often entertained the notion that unwellness leads to an irrevocable showdown with surrender. In letting go of what can't be controlled, I find that faith's role becomes imperative in sustaining the heart's own intelligence.

Journal entry:

Having once again asked the divine Entities and Spirits of light for guidance in desiring to become more attuned to the visions that will best suit my continued awakening I've almost instantaneously received them. Reflecting on why I came to the Casa in the first place...hope and faith that there was a greater healing force in the universe...I now return to its nourishing source to try and surrender my desire for control and need to know to the ineffable ways of Source.

I'm now experiencing a great calm and peace wash over my entire being. Clearly there is a divine plan. I can either continue fighting it or let go and free up my energy to use in my healing. I see the inclination in myself and those around me to want to control their destinies at almost any cost and I'm struck with the realization it just doesn't work that way. There's a certain bliss in the act of what I've come to call "knowing surrender." Can I maintain this intention?

In reality, since learning I'd manifested this malady my *real* battles have been with my imperious, often intractable ego telling me "it" is right, not my heart-mind. I've come to view consciousness as a bridge spanning the gap between notional patterns of engaging life and new, self-affirming behaviors that more readily support the pursuit of *actuality*. The trick is achieving peaceful coexistence between ego and higher self.

The heightened *awareness* that illness delivered into the midst of my lifelong "acting-out" represented a critical step toward the embrace of behaviors, choices and mindsets opposite to those based in the falsity and illusion I'd originally chosen. In retrospect the arrival of dis-ease in my physical form was anti-climactic. I was already ill many, many years before a quantifiable sickness actually materialized. Illness was created through behaviors at odds with the truth of my deepest authenticity. A brief yet poignant journal entry expresses my burgeoning awareness at having contributed to the emergence of dis-ease.

Journal entry:

...and so I'd say nothing, hoping like hell the problem would disappear, then internalize my anger when it failed to go away, seething from every pore at my failure to control what I felt had to be controlled. This failure to speak-internalizing-of-anger-loss-of-control loop has been an immense issue for me.

In urging myself towards truth I spelunked through my own deepest caverns, those sanctum sanctorums within, hiding the private, raw pain only I knew intimately. Gently, the occult was tugged into the light of self-scrutiny, fears were peeled back to expose my humanness in all of its perfect imperfection, my soul was given permission to voice its most profound longing for the very first time since entering physical form.

At that place where faith intersects with an examined life *everything becomes possible.* As all the pieces of the puzzle were falling into place, the way that I engaged life naturally began to change. The way I occupied my new state of challenge altered, as if on cue, moving from non-self-empowering choices to distinguishing what was *real* and what was *illusion,* between what mattered and what was of no lasting consequence. The pentimento of lacerations to my inherent truth, which formed like scar tissue over a repeatedly damaged heart, was finally peeled back, layer by layer, exposing my disconnection from wholeness. Once I owned the truth of that story I could take back possession of my legitimacy.

When I was a young boy I seemed able to see things others failed to observe. These phenomena were very important to me, backlit by some clarifying illumination, as if not being acknowledged might invalidate their existence…or even my own. Seeing as a child sees means observing the unfolding continuum of life without filters, vitally aware of the prayer it speaks to us in whispers under its breath. As children we viscerally engage with this susurrus of Spirit, for our play is an invocation of our truth at its most elementary level.

For most of us gaining adulthood means forsaking the awe and wonder with which we met life when young. If this guileless way of seeing the world in its truth, in its real and actual beingness, is allowed to lie fallow or wither away, we stand to lose a precious facet of our soul, which determines the fullness of who we become. Far from being a hindrance, childlike awe is akin to reverence, an ally in helping us uncover the enigma of our place in the grand design.

As my odyssey unfolded I rediscovered the means to reconnect with this manner of *sensing* the world. I use the word *sensing* to connote full employment of the physical sense apparatus along with those *extrasensory* ways of perceiving this and other realities. Each of us possesses many additional means of knowing life than we think. By reconnecting in this manner with the guileless manner

I once employed to view life, I validated my place within a larger context of truth.

• • •

Growing up, I modeled myself after my father's non-confrontational persona, adopting it as my own, striking a conciliatory pose in any situation where the odor of conflict wafted redolently on the breeze. I abhorred confrontation and sought out all available means to distance myself from it...a virtual impossibility in a house where the presence of six boys brought fuller, testosterone-fueled significance to the word *cacophony.*

Due to my empathic sensitivity I *felt* in a very potent way what others emoted. *Feeling* the vibrations of others' anger, consternation and impatience in such a tactile manner, I concluded they were aimed at me. I felt the sheer strength of these emotions in my energy field and I felt it in my bones. It was simultaneously a physical *and* a visceral sensation.

That I possessed such low self-esteem conspired with the sheer force of these sensations to offer scant persuasion such emotions weren't directed at me. The net effect was a child who *sensed* feelings intensely and frequently grew overwhelmed by the discord of such psychic attunement.

As a result, control became my raison d'etre from a very young age. It became my quest and my sole focus, the one constant in a world otherwise as uncertain as my own emotional equilibrium. Not ironically, it was the primary reason I found such success in the business world as a negotiator, for I'd already learned early in life just what it took to soothe the savage beast.

I'd lost the ability to interact through the vehicle of voice, discovering in its place the new idiom of the written word. Dialogue always allowed me to hide behind words, to manipulate them and the situations over whose control I sought dominance. In being deprived of speech I was forced to carefully consider what I wanted to say and why I wanted to say it, as the effort required to extract discernible words from my voicebox or peck them out laboriously with my one good typing finger often superseded the importance of the attempted message. I came to see this process as a watershed element in coming to grips with how I'd disingenuously viewed the world. Reclaiming the truth of my inner voice grew out of this awareness. The irony that my inner voice was only discovered in the act of losing my physical voice was a reminder that gifts sometimes come wrapped in chaos.

Like the insight that art provided, the act of writing brought me to direct confrontation with the truth of my original dispossesion...the sad product of a frightened, lost child...and to the means of changing it. Through the process of self-discovery that writing offered, I reclaimed parts of myself all but lost in long-held resistance to the light that integrity repeatedly tried to cast on my world of pathological shadows. I saw my original wounding as the point of entry for my pain as well as the point of departure from it, in a return to increasing levels of wellness.

As I move deeper into my newly illumined life I'm intent on striking an equitable balance between letting go of the control I've spent years stockpiling while continuing to embrace the lessons ushered in by illness. I will walk again one day. One day I will speak again. All my efforts in continually toiling at the work of healing my mind, emotions and behaviors remain pointed in that direction.

To those used to accepting western medicine's prevailing paradigm concerning "terminal" disease, the preceding will only serve to further convict me of wishful thinking, outright denial if not arrogant presumptuousness. On the other hand, for those possessed of a broader respect for and faith in the presence of miracles, my journey serves to confirm the undeniable presence of God in my transformative awakening and cure.

In the meantime the Entities of the Casa de Dom Inacio continue healing me, while supporting *my* intentions and *my* continuing efforts to mend what *I'm* responsible for, taking care of *my* part in the cure. When I've done enough personal work and arrive at a point where I merit regaining lost functions, they'll be restored. While the loving ministrations of the Entities support me every step of the way, their ability to instantly heal me outright will never supersede or interfere with my soul's obligation to remedy that for which I alone am responsible.

What is a miracle? Is it the divine manifesting its perfection and order in the world through the restorative medium of unconditional love? Or are miracles natural acts of the universe we simply don't understand, based on scientific-spiritual facts as yet undiscovered? Miracles are, at an intrinsic level, derived from perception. One person's observation of a supernatural act isn't supportable as such by another. When some people look for the miraculous they seem able to find its presence everywhere. They expect it, anticipate it, believe in it. For others, the concept of anything heaven-sent is as ludicrous as the notion of a supreme being. The gap between blind acceptance of everything as miraculous and the blind refusal to treat unexplainable phenomena as anything more than anecdotal and apocryphal is narrowing.

The many years I spent living the lie that errant feelings seduced me into believing about myself brought me to the realization that, at all costs, love coming through the channel of an open heart is the *only* answer. It is a universal panacea, the antidote to all fear. When each one of us believes in this power *and it becomes the sole motivating force driving our intentions* love will cease being an idealized, grandiose sentiment and come to exist as a statement of transformative fact. In such an environment the world will continually pulsate with miracles.

Anything occurring outside the boundaries of one's understanding proves insufficient at explaining such phenomena because they provide no basis on which to conceptualize what's been observed. Once I'd learned how to get out of my constantly analyzing head and into my heart-mind, the need for empirical proof lessened dramatically. My perceptions underwent radical restructuring, which no longer relied on blind faith, but instead were illuminated by acknowledging the existence of mystery as a transcending element of natural order. I've personally experienced many events that can't be accounted for from a rational perspective. These required that I grow my intuitive intelligence to decipher the message each contained.

Coming to the understanding that the heart already contains the five senses as well as vast extra-sensory capabilities allows this radical shift in awareness. You no longer need accept as conventional wisdom that the mind is for thinking and the heart solely for feeling. In fact the heart-mind is an organ of rational intention melded with higher vibrations only accessible through the love it contains. Its existence is a living metaphor for the pulse of emotion that guides its direction, propelling each conjured thought literally into form. Its *mind* is vastly more discerning than any level of learning attained by even the most advanced intellect. It's intuitive and psychically attuned, drawing on wisdom accrued across millennia. Heart-mind *knows* to an extent incapable of being experienced by mere mind. For heart-mind contains mere mind in its midst.

Drawing on my own history I saw how conscious choice is as intentional as unconscious choice. This means you choose by not choosing…as I'd done the better part of my life. Either selection brings the consequence of your intention into a tangible form of matter. Thus you *are* precisely what you think, feel and believe even as your choices manifest as concrete forms shaped by the impressions, sentiments and opinions you hold as truth. The aphorism "be careful what you think" swells with significance when viewed from the perspective of creating reality out of consciousness. We create reality through our thoughts while those same thoughts are empowered by the impetus of our feelings. As the poet Rumi offered, "We become these words we say…."

Believing in my healing allowed me to dream it literally into existence. My desire to survive was so profound, its energy created a potent vision of wellness in my mind, bathing it with salutary nurture, allowing little room for anything else. Believing in love for the first time allowed love to fill my long vacant heart. I learned love is *the* most profound healing energy in existence. Without the Entities patiently leading me to one epiphany after another, none of this would've happened.

I'd also come to understand the difficulty in trying to explain my transcendent/transpersonal experiences in language ill-suited to describing the numinous. If there's no common touchstone with others who've experienced similar journeys, any attempts at dialogue become stymied, creating incredulous looks but little else. Add to this an absence of belief and faith in what can't always be readily understood and explained, and the tendency is to allow disbelief and fear a toe-hold in the mind and heart.

What I'd experienced inside non-conforming reality didn't lend itself to dissemination through any language I was in command of. While bits and pieces of each event shared common expression in the emotions they elicited, taken as a whole these incidents lay outside the rational concepts one customarily employs to describe his or her surroundings. If there was anything resembling a *numenclature* common to my experiences, it was a wholly non-rational, experiential language without vocabulary where what one encountered mystically wasn't readily translatable into common prose. It was a private arena of awakening and discernment.

• • •

EVEN AS THE spirit Entities of the Casa de Dom Inacio continue their work at turning off the disease's switch deep in my genetic code, I, too, will continue to draw into conscious awareness those as yet unfulfilled aspects of my thoughts and feelings that require more knowing light. Together we will overcome the seemingly incurable and in the process demonstrate the power of love, faith and perseverance to heal *any* affliction.

As with any team effort, different individuals have different responsibilities. While I'm clear regarding what role my Spirit tutors play in the cure, my own efforts continually undergo transformation as I receive new insights. I like to think of my day as one long conversation with the potent forces in Spirit comprised of my guides and mentors. A petition I recite innumerable times daily is, "show me how to learn to more fully help myself." This prayer evolved out of the growing understanding that without being *completely* answerable for my own part in the healing equation, how could I continually ask Spirit for their help? What was crucial I learned was the utter accountability I had to my cure. Over time it became very clear my participation in doing what needed to be done to promote self-healing was proportionate to what I'd receive from the Entities.

After hearing the Entity say he'd cure me I was anxious to be given some kind of timetable for my return to the ranks of the uncompromised. At one point in the early years of my challenge I asked the Entity when I'd finally be freed from disability's shackles to walk and talk again. He answered me with a succinct "that depends." Still buried within my epic self-generated unconsciousness, I failed to grasp what could've easily followed his two word reply: "on you." As my fog gradually lifted and I began to see what had always been right in front of me, a frisson of epiphany passed through me, leaving those two sagely omitted words lodged in my awareness.

Today, armed with greater perspective and a far different mindset, I freely confide that I don't know how long my healing odyssey will take. It may be that I detect improvement in my physical form very soon. After all I've already experienced quantifiable physical amelioration a number of times since first seeking treatment from the spirit Entities at the Casa de Dom Inacio. In addition, the healing that's taken shape in my emotional, mental and spiritual bodies has been enormous.

Equally possible is that my body's return to homeostasis may unfold over the remainder of my life. After all my life journey is a *process* as unfinished, imperfect and rough around the edges, as that mirrored by my soul's own experiential progression across many lifetimes already lived. In the intervening time I'm given to work on my spiritual evolution, I'm assured ample opportunity of being tested in my patience and faith. I'm also certain I'll find more reasons to continue trusting in the unseen forces that have shaped my cure from the start.

In the last analysis, my miracle isn't confined to a point in time when my physical organism regains its purchase on equilibrium. For while the seed of that providential blessing continues germinating inside, I recognize a far more remarkable translation taking shape in the core of my heart. Healing can be described as "tending to cure or restore to health." If that is so, then the unburdening and cleansing of the center of emotional sentiment within my being…inside my heart…acts as the true fulcrum for all the extraordinary change I've experienced to this point in my odyssey.

Some might say that this emotional restoration hardly qualifies as an event worthy of the term "miraculous," but when you're in denial of the truth of your emotions as long as I'd been in my non-self-examined life, in my *beforeness*, you have to question whether the miracle of being cured of an incurable disease takes precedence over the cure undertaken by opening a closed heart. In fact, is one precipitated by the other?

As significant and unprecedented as are the levels of healing I've already experienced, the evolution of my miracle doesn't hinge on some future moment when all in my life has been restored to an ideal state. The journey itself…now *living* in this joy-filled, self-examined moment…holds the greatest poignancy and engenders the most profound gratitude.

The End

12640939R00133